OXFORD
UNIVERSITY PRESS

fourth edition

English File

Beginner

Student's Book

WITH ONLINE PRACTICE

Christina Latham-Koenig
Clive Oxenden
Jerry Lambert

Paul Seligson and Clive Oxenden
are the original co-authors of
English File 1 and *English File 2*

Contents

Course overview

English File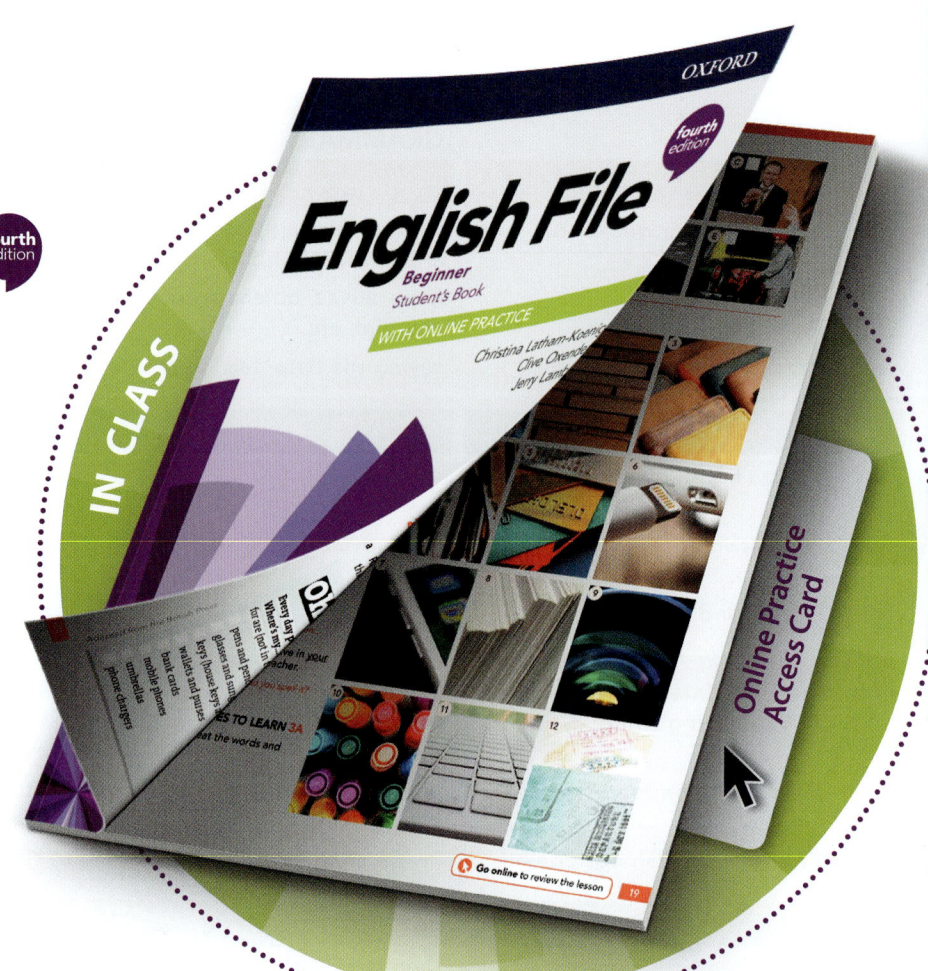

Welcome to **English File fourth edition**. This is how to use the Student's Book, Online Practice, and the Workbook in and out of class.

Student's Book

All the language and skills you need to improve your English, with Grammar, Vocabulary, Pronunciation, and skills work in every File. Also available as an eBook.

Use your Student's Book in class with your teacher.

Workbook

Grammar, Vocabulary, and Pronunciation practice for every lesson.

Use your Workbook for homework or for self-study to practise language and to check your progress.

Go to **englishfileonline.com** and use the code on your Access Card to log into the Online Practice.

ACTIVITIES AUDIO VIDEO RESOURCES

ONLINE

LOOK AGAIN

- Review the language from every lesson.
- Watch the videos and listen to all the class audio as many times as you like.

PRACTICE

- Improve your skills with extra Reading, Writing, Listening, and Speaking practice.
- Use the interactive video to practise Practical English.

CHECK YOUR PROGRESS

- Test yourself on the language from the File and get instant feedback.
- Try an extra Challenge.

SOUND BANK

- Use the Sound Bank videos to practise and improve your pronunciation of English sounds.

Online Practice

Look again at Student's Book language you want to review or that you missed in class, do extra *Practice* activities, and *Check your progress* on what you've learnt so far.

Use the Online Practice to learn outside the classroom and get instant feedback on your progress.

englishfileonline.com

Hi, I'm Helen.

Hello, I'm Tom. Nice to meet you.

G verb *be* (singular): *I* and *you* **V** numbers 0–10, days of the week, saying goodbye **P** /h/, /aɪ/, and /iː/

1 LISTENING & SPEAKING

a ◉1.2 Read and listen.

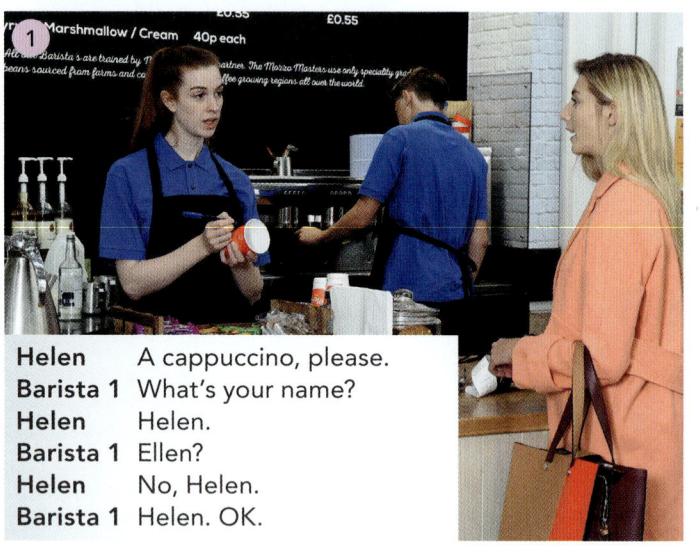

Helen	A cappuccino, please.
Barista 1	What's your name?
Helen	Helen.
Barista 1	Ellen?
Helen	No, Helen.
Barista 1	Helen. OK.

Barista 2	Are you Diana?
Helen	No, I'm not. I'm Helen.
Barista 2	Sorry.
	Helen? Your cappuccino.
Helen	Thanks.

Tom	Hello. Are you Helen?
Helen	Yes, I am. And you're Tom.
Tom	Yes! Nice to meet you.
Helen	Nice to meet you.
Tom	Just a minute.

Tom	Hi. A tea, please.
Barista 1	OK. What's your name?
Tom	Tom.
Barista 1	Dom. A tea.
Tom	No, I'm Tom, not Dom.

b ◉1.3 Listen and repeat the conversations.

c In pairs, practise the conversations.

2 GRAMMAR verb *be* (singular): *I* and *you*

a Write *I* or *You* in photos 1 and 2.

b **G** p.92 **Grammar Bank 1A**

c ◉1.6 Listen and say the contractions.

1 ◉) *I am* (*I'm*

_____'m Helen.

_____'re Tom.

3 VOCABULARY numbers 0–10

a 🔊 **1.7** Listen and tick (✓) the correct photo.

1 ▢

2 ▢

3 ▢

b Ⓥ **p.116 Vocabulary Bank** Numbers
Do Part 1.

c 🔊 **1.9** Listen and write the numbers.

7								

d 🔊 **1.10** Listen and say the next number.

🔊 *one, two* (*three*

4 PRONUNCIATION
/h/, /aɪ/, and /iː/

a 🔊 **1.11** Listen and repeat the words and sounds.

🏠	**h**ouse	**h**i **h**ello **H**elen
🚲	b**i**ke	**I'**m n**i**ce f**i**ve n**i**ne
🌳	tr**ee**	m**ee**t thr**ee** t**ea** pl**ea**se

b 🔊 **1.12** Listen and repeat the sentences.
Hello, Helen!
Hi, I'm Mike.
Three teas, please.

5 SPEAKING

Practise with other students.

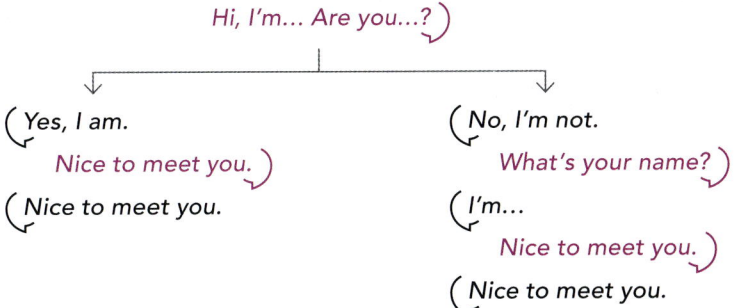

Hi, I'm... Are you...?

Yes, I am.
Nice to meet you.
Nice to meet you.

No, I'm not.
What's your name?
I'm...
Nice to meet you.
Nice to meet you.

6 VOCABULARY
days of the week, saying goodbye

a 🔊 **1.13** Listen and repeat the days of the week.

<u>Mon</u>day /ˈmʌndeɪ/
<u>Tues</u>day /ˈtjuːzdeɪ/
<u>Wednes</u>day /ˈwenzdeɪ/
<u>Thurs</u>day /ˈθɜːzdeɪ/
<u>Fri</u>day /ˈfraɪdeɪ/
<u>Satur</u>day /ˈsætədeɪ/
<u>Sun</u>day /ˈsʌndeɪ/

🔍 **Capital letters**
Monday **NOT** ~~monday~~
Friday **NOT** ~~friday~~

b Write the days of the week.
to<u>day</u> = _____   to<u>morrow</u> = _____
the week<u>end</u> = _____ and _____

c Cover **a** and say the days from Monday to Sunday. What days are <u>your</u> English classes?

d 🔊 **1.14** Listen and repeat.

Goodbye, Tom. See you on Friday.

Bye.

e Say goodbye.   (*Bye. See you tomorrow.*

WORDS AND PHRASES TO LEARN 1A

p.131 Listen and repeat the words and phrases.

🔄 **Go online** to review the lesson

1B World music

G verb *be* (singular): *he, she, it*   V countries   P /ɪ/, /əʊ/, /s/, and /ʃ/

1 VOCABULARY countries

a 🔊 1.16 Listen to the music. Where's it from? Write 1–5.

☐ China   ☐ England   1 Spain   ☐ the United States   ☐ Turkey

b 🔊 1.17 Listen and check.

c **V** p.117 **Vocabulary Bank** Countries and nationalities Do Part 1.

d 🔊 1.19 Listen and repeat the conversation. Copy the rhythm.

> **A Where** are you **from**?
> **B** I'm from **To**le**do**.
> **A Where's To**le**do**?
> **B** It's in **Spain**.

e Practise the conversation with your city and country.

f **C Communication** Where is it? **A** p.78 **B** p.82 Ask and answer questions about cities and countries.

2 GRAMMAR verb *be* (singular): *he, she, it*

a 🔊 1.20 Listen to the conversation. Write the countries.

> A Wow! Caetano Veloso!
> B Where's he from?
> A He's from _____.
> B Is Lila Downs from _____, too?
> A No, she isn't. She's from _____.
> B Is she good?
> A Yes, she is. Very good.

b 🔊 1.21 Listen again and repeat.

c In pairs, practise the conversation.

d Match the words with the photos.

☐ she
☐ it
☐ he

e Complete the chart for *be* (singular).

⊞	⊟
I am = I'm	I am not = I'm not
you are = you're	you are not = you aren't
he is = he____	he is not = he ____
she is = she____	she is not = she ____
it is = it____	it is not = it ____

f **G p.92 Grammar Bank 1B**

Where's he from?

He's from Brazil.

June 18–19

WORLD MUSIC FESTIVAL

FRIDAY 18
Caetano Veloso

SATURDAY 19
Lila Downs

ALSO APPEARING
Lula Pena
Mercedes Peón
Gaye Su Akyol
Sergio Mendoza
Warsaw Village Band
Martynas Levickis

3 PRONUNCIATION /ɪ/, /əʊ/, /s/, and /ʃ/

a ◖))1.25 Listen and repeat the words and sounds.

🐟	**fish**	it Italy six England
☎	**phone**	no don't Poland Mexico know
🐍	**snake**	say seven city nice
∫	**shower**	she Russia

b ◖))1.26 Listen and repeat the sentences.

Is he from Italy?   It's a nice city.
I don't know.   She's from Russia.

4 LISTENING & SPEAKING

a ◖))1.27 Listen to the difference between *he* and *she*.

1 a Is he from Egypt?   b Is she from Egypt?
2 a He's from Turkey.   b She's from Turkey.
3 a Where's he from?   b Where's she from?
4 a He's nice.   b She's nice.
5 a Where is he?   b Where is she?

b Practise saying sentences a and b.

c ◖))1.28 Listen and tick (✓) the sentence you hear in a.

d ◖))1.29 Listen and write six sentences or questions.

1 *He's from Egypt.*

e Look at the photos. Ask and answer questions with a partner about the artists or instruments.

Where's he from? ⟩ ⟨ He's from the USA.

Where's she from? ⟩ ⟨ She's from Spain.

Where's it from? ⟩ ⟨ It's from Russia.

f ◖))1.30 Listen and check.

g Test your partner. Point to a photo and ask a question with *Is he / she / it from…?*

Number two. Is she from Japan? ⟩

⟨ No, she isn't. She's from China.

WORDS AND PHRASES TO LEARN 1B

p.131 Listen and repeat the words and phrases.

Go online to review the lesson

Practical English How do you spell it?

1 THE ALPHABET

a 🔊 1.32 Listen to the alphabet. Repeat the letters.

Aa Bb Cc Dd
Ee Ff Gg Hh
Ii Jj Kk Ll
Mm Nn Oo Pp
Qq Rr Ss Tt
Uu Vv Ww
Xx Yy Zz

b 🔊 1.33 Listen and repeat the words, sounds, and letters.

🌳	tr**ee**	B C D E G P T V
🥚	**e**gg	F L M N S X
🚂	tr**ai**n	A H J K

c 🔊 1.34 Listen to the difference between the letters.

1	E	A	7	G J
2	E	I	8	K Q
3	U	W	9	M N
4	Y	I	10	S C
5	B	P	11	D T
6	B	V	12	W V

d 🔊 1.35 Listen. (Circle) the letter you hear in **c**.

e 🔊 1.36 Look at the photos. How do you say the letters? Listen and check.

f 🌐 **Communication** Hit the ships **A** p.78 **B** p.82
Play a game with numbers and letters.

2 VOCABULARY the classroom

a 🔊 1.37 Listen and complete the conversation with the words from the list.

Book	English	spell	What

Student	[1]_____'s *libro* in [2]_____?
Teacher	[3]_____.
Student	How do you [4]_____ it?
Teacher	B-O-O-K.

b 🟢 **V** p.118 **Vocabulary Bank** The classroom

c Complete the conversations.

1	Teacher	_____ your books, please. _____ to page 7.
	Student	_____, can you _____ that, please?
	Teacher	Go to page 7.

2	Student	_____ me. _____ do you spell 'birthday'?
	Teacher	B-I-R-T-H-D-A-Y.

3	Student	_____ I'm late.
	Teacher	That's OK. Sit _____, please.

d 🔊 1.40 Listen and check.

e In pairs, practise the conversations in **c**.

f 🔊 1.41 Listen and do the actions.

1 🔊 *Stand up.*

3 ▶ CHECKING INTO A HOTEL

a 🔊 **1.42** Watch or listen to Rob. Circle a or b.

1 Rob is from _____.
  a the UK
  b the USA
2 He's _____.
  a an artist
  b a journalist
3 He's in Poland _____.
  a on holiday
  b for work

b 🔊 **1.43** Watch or listen and order the sentences.

7	W-A-L-K-E-R.
	My name's Rob Walker. I have a reservation.
	Sorry?
1	Hello.
	How do you spell it?
	Walker.
	Sorry, what's your surname?
	Thank you. OK, Mr Walker. You're in room 321.
	Good afternoon.
	W-A-L-K-E-R.
	Thanks.

> 🔍 **Names**
> **name**   Rob Walker
> **first name**   Rob
> **surname (or last name)** Walker

c 🔊 **1.44** Watch or listen and repeat the conversation.

d In pairs, role-play the conversation. Use your name and surname.

> 🔍 **Greetings**
> Good <u>mor</u>ning   » 12.00
> Good after<u>noon</u>   12.00 » 6.00 p.m.
> Good <u>eve</u>ning   6.00 p.m. »

4 ▶ BOOKING A TABLE

a 🔊 **1.45** Watch or listen to Jenny. Circle a or b.

1 Jenny's from _____.
  a the USA
  b the UK
2 _____ is her birthday.
  a Today
  b Tomorrow
3 Locanda Verde is a _____.
  a restaurant
  b club

b 🔊 **1.46** Watch or listen and complete the information.

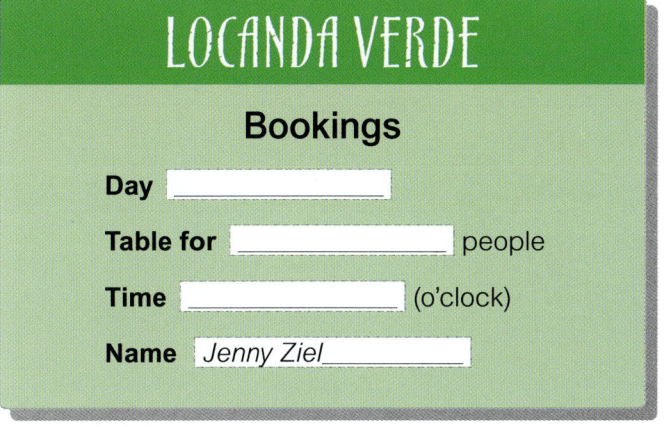

LOCANDA VERDE
Bookings

Day _____

Table for _____ people

Time _____ (o'clock)

Name *Jenny Ziel_____*

> 🔍 **Z**
> In the USA, Z = zee /ziː/
> In the UK, Z = zed /zed/

5 ▶ USEFUL PHRASES

🔊 **1.47** Watch or listen and repeat the useful phrases.

I have a reservation.	Good morning.
How do you spell it?	How can I help you?
Sorry?	A table for tomorrow, please.
Thank you.	That's right.

> **Go online** to watch the video and review the lesson

2A Are you on holiday?

> Are you American?
>
> No, we aren't. We're from Canada.

G verb *be* (plural): *we, you, they* **V** nationalities **P** /dʒ/, /tʃ/, and /ʃ/

1 VOCABULARY nationalities

a Look at the photos and circle the nationality words.

b Write the countries for each photo.

1 *Turkey* 2 _____
3 _____ 4 _____

c **V** p.117 Vocabulary Bank Countries and nationalities Do Part 2.

2 PRONUNCIATION /dʒ/, /tʃ/, and /ʃ/

a 🔊 2.2 Listen and repeat the words and sounds.

🎵 dʒ	**j**azz	**J**apan **G**ermany **E**gypt
🐭 tʃ	**ch**ess	**Ch**inese Fren**ch**
🚿 ʃ	**sh**ower	**Sp**anish **P**olish E**gyp**tian

> 🔍 **Sounds**
> The letter *j* = /dʒ/, e.g. **J**apan /dʒəˈpæn/.
> The letter *g* = /dʒ/, e.g. **G**ermany /ˈdʒɜːməni/ or /g/, e.g. **g**o /gəʊ/.

b 🔊 2.3 Listen and repeat the sentences.
He isn't from Egypt, he's German.
It isn't French, it's Chinese.
She isn't Spanish, she's Polish.

c 🔊 2.4 Listen. Say the nationality.

1 ») *I'm from China.* (*He's Chinese.*

2 ») *I'm from Spain.* (*She's Spanish.*

3 GRAMMAR verb *be* (plural): *we, you, they*

a Read the conversation. Complete it with words from the list.

> American are aren't English I'm meet sit Thanks

E KING'S ARMS

Jessica Excuse me. Are they free?
Charles Yes, they ¹*are*. Please ²_____ down.
Jessica ³_____. I'm Jessica. Hi.
Jim And ⁴_____ Jim.
Charles Are you ⁵_____?
Jessica No, we ⁶_____. We're from Canada.
Charles Oh, OK! We're ⁷_____. I'm Charles.
Rachel And I'm Rachel.
Jim Nice to ⁸_____ you.

b 🔊 2.5 Listen and check. Then complete the chart.

be (plural)	
+	**−**
we are = we*'re*	we are not = we *aren't*
you are = you_____	you are not = you _____
they are = they_____	they are not = they _____

c **G** p.94 Grammar Bank 2A

d 🔊 2.9 Listen. Ask the questions.

1 ») *You're Chinese.* (*Are you Chinese?*

2 ») *We're late.* (*Are we late?*

4 READING & LISTENING

a 🔊 **2.10** Read and listen to the conversation. Then number the pictures 1–5.

Jessica	Where in England are you from?
Charles	We're from here, from Oxford.
Jim	Oxford's a beautiful city!
Rachel	Yes, it is. Are you on holiday?
Jim	No, we aren't, we're on business. But today's a free day.
Jessica	Yes, we're tourists today! Ooh. What's that?
Jim	Oh… Are they your dogs?
Charles	Yes, they are. Sit. Sit!
Jessica	They're very nice. But I'm not very good with dogs.
Jim	Look – a free table. Over there.
Jessica	Nice to meet you. Have a nice day.
Charles	Thanks. Nice to meet you, too.
Rachel	Bye. Good dogs, good dogs.

A ☐

B ☐

C ☐

D ☐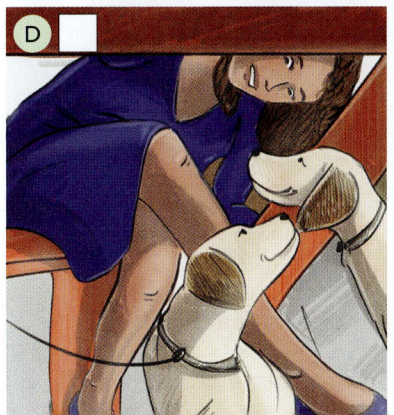

E ☐

b Read the conversation again. Write short answers.

1 Are Rachel and Charles from the USA?
No, _____.

2 Are Jessica and Jim on business?
_____

3 Is today a free day for Jessica and Jim?
_____

4 Is Jessica good with dogs?
_____

c 🔊 **2.11** Listen and complete the phrases.

1 Excuse me. Are they _____?
2 Are you on _____?
3 We're on _____.
4 What's _____?
5 Have a nice _____!
6 Nice to meet you, _____.

d In groups of four, practise the conversations in **3a** and **4a**.

5 SPEAKING

a Ask and answer the questions with a partner.

1 Is Pedro Almodóvar Spanish?

Yes, he is. / No, he isn't. / I don't know.

2 Are Chow Chow dogs Russian?
3 Is Lufthansa German?
4 Is Emma Watson American?

b 🅒 **Communication** Is sushi Chinese?
A p.78 B p.82 Ask and answer about different nationalities.

WORDS AND PHRASES TO LEARN 2A

p.131 Listen and repeat the words and phrases.

Go online to review the lesson

What's your phone number?

It's 07710 097456.

| G Wh- and How questions with be | V phone numbers, numbers 11–100 | P understanding numbers |

1 READING & LISTENING

a 🔊 2.13 Read and listen to the conversation. Then complete the information on the card.

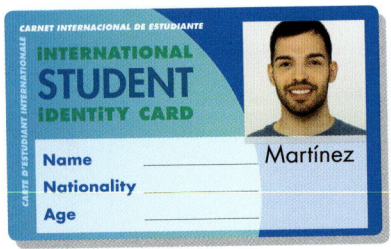

CARNET INTERNACIONAL DE ESTUDIANTE

INTERNATIONAL STUDENT IDENTITY CARD

CARTE D'ETUDIANT INTERNATIONALE

Martínez

Name _____
Nationality _____
Age _____

Pia	Who's he?
Lin	He's Alex. He's in my class.
Pia	Where's he from?
Lin	He's from Mexico.
Pia	How old is he?
Lin	He's 22, I think.
Pia	He's very good-looking!

English Centre Reception

b 🔊 2.14 Listen and complete the conversation.

ENTRANCE

Lin	Hi, Pia. How are you?
Pia	Hi, Lin. I'm fine, and you?
Lin	I'm fine, too. This is Alex. He's in my ¹_____. Alex, this is Pia.
Pia	Hi, Alex!
Alex	Hi. ²_____ class are you in?

Lin	That's my bus! Bye. See you ³_____!
Alex	Bye. ⁴_____ are you from, Pia?
Pia	I'm from ⁵_____. This is my bus stop. Bye, Alex. Nice to meet you.
Alex	Nice to meet you, too, Pia. What's your ⁶_____ number?
Pia	Sorry, my bus… It's 07365…!

REGENT ST 94

23 73 94

c 🔊 2.15 Listen and repeat the conversation. Then practise it in groups of three.

2 GRAMMAR Wh- and How questions with be

a 🔊 2.16 Listen and repeat the question words.

How   What   Where   Who

b Complete the chart with question words from **a**.

1	A _Where_ are you from?	B I'm from Germany.
2	A _____ are you?	B Fine, thanks.
3	A _____ 's he?	B He's a friend.
4	A _____ 's your name?	B Molly.
5	A _____ 's Modena?	B It's in Italy.
6	A _____ old are you?	B 26.
7	A _____ 's your phone number?	B 07702 960836.

c 🔊 2.17 Listen and check.

d 🌐 p.94 Grammar Bank 2B

e Cover the questions in the chart in **b** and look at the answers. Say the questions.

3 VOCABULARY phone numbers, numbers 11–100

a 🔊 2.19 Listen and complete the phone number.

0		0			9	9	0		

b 🔊 2.20 Practise saying these phone numbers. Listen and check.

1 `028 901 80361`

2 `08081 570724`

3 `0131 496 0638`

c Ask and answer with a partner. Write the number.

⌒ *What's your phone number?*

d 🔊 p.116 **Vocabulary Bank** Numbers Do Part 2.

e 🔊 2.23 Listen and write the numbers.

15											

f Play *Buzz*.

4 PRONUNCIATION & LISTENING understanding numbers

a 🔊 2.24 Listen to the difference between the numbers.

1 a **13** b **30**   5 a **17** b **70**
2 a **14** b **40**   6 a **18** b **80**
3 a **15** b **50**   7 a **19** b **90**
4 a **16** b **60**

b 🔊 2.25 Listen. Which number do you hear? Ⓒircle a or b in **a**. Then practise saying all the numbers.

c 🔊 2.26 Listen to the conversations. Number the questions 1–4.

☐ What's your address?   ☐ What's your email?
☐ How old are you?   ☐ What's your phone number?

d Listen again and write the numbers in the answers.

1 ✆ _____
2 _____ King Street
3 Age: _____
4 james_____@ukmail.com

┌─────────────────────────────┐
│ 🔍 **Email addresses**   │
│   @ = at   . = dot   │
└─────────────────────────────┘

5 WRITING & SPEAKING

a Ⓦ p.86 **Writing** A form Complete an online form.

b Ⓒ**Communication** Personal information A p.79 B p.83 Interview your partner.

6 ▶ VIDEO LISTENING Meet the students

a Watch the video *Meet the students*. Is it a nice school?

b Watch again. Ⓒircle the correct answer.

1 Alicia is in *Brighton / Bournemouth* today.
2 She *is / isn't* on holiday.
3 Rike and Hyeongwoo are *teachers / students*.
4 Hyeongwoo is *23 / 26* years old.
5 His teacher is *Stephen / Laura*.
6 Rike is *German / Swiss*.
7 Laura is a good *teacher / student*.
8 Their student house *is / isn't* near the school.

c Watch some extracts from the video. Complete the sentences with words from the list.

bedrooms big canteen computer room
garden kitchen small south

1 Brighton is in the _____ of England.
2 It's a _____ school with about 350 students.
3 His class is _____, with only five students.
4 ...they're in the _____...or here in the _____.
5 It's a big house with five _____, a _____, and a _____.

WORDS AND PHRASES TO LEARN 2B

p.131 Listen and repeat the words and phrases.

 Go online to watch the video and review the lesson

GRAMMAR

Circle a or b.

_____ 's your name?
a Who   b **What**

1 _____ you from Italy?
  a Are   b Is

2 _____ Lisa. I'm Marisa.
  a Am not   b I'm not

3 Hi, Mark! _____ in my class.
  a You   b You're

4 A _____ from?
  B I'm from Russia.
  a Where are you   b Where you are

5 A Where's Gdansk?
  B _____ in Poland.
  a Is   b It's

6 A Is John married?
  B No, _____.
  a he isn't   b she isn't

7 A _____ English?
  B No, she's American.
  a She's   b Is she

8 They _____ Spanish. They're Mexican.
  a aren't   b not

9 A Are you on holiday?
  B No, _____ on business.
  a we're   b we

10 Ana and Julia are from Recife. _____
   Brazilian.
   a She's   b They're

11 A _____ Mario and Renata Italian?
   B Yes, they're from Milan.
   a Are   b Is

12 A How old _____?
   B I'm 19.
   a you are   b are you

13 A _____ are you?
   B Fine, thanks. And you?
   a How   b Who

14 A _____ address?
   B It's 304 High Street.
   a What your   b What's your

15 A How _____ your surname?
   B G-A-R-C-I-A.
   a you spell   b do you spell

VOCABULARY

a Complete the chart.

Country	Nationality
China	Chinese
Turkey	1 _____
2 _____	Swiss
the United States	3 _____
4 _____	English
5 _____	Egyptian
Japan	6 _____

b Write the next number or word.

one, two, _three_
1 zero, one, _____
2 five, six, _____
3 eleven, twelve, _____
4 nineteen, twenty, _____
5 Tuesday, Wednesday, _____
6 Friday, Saturday, _____

c Complete the words.

Where are you **fr**_om_?
1 Good morning. **O**_____ your books, please. Page 19.
2 A **S**_____ I'm late.
  B OK. Sit **d**_____.
3 A What's the answer to number 10?
  B I don't **kn**_____.
4 A Excuse **m**_____, **wh**_____ _plato_ in English?
  B Plate.
  A Can you **r**_____ that, please?
  B Yes. Plate.
5 A What's your phone **n**_____?
  B 029 2018 0583.
  A Thanks. What's your **e**_____?
  B It's tom@hotmail.com.

d Write the things in the classroom.

a dictionary

1 _____   2 _____   3 _____   4 _____

PRONUNCIATION

a Write the words for the sound pictures.

 *bike*

1	(tree)		3	(fish)
2	(phone)		4	(computer)
			5	(waterfall)

b 🅿 **p.134–5 Sound Bank** Look at more words with the sounds in **a**, and these sounds:

Practise saying the example words.

c Underline the stressed syllable.

Sa|tur|day
1 Chi|nese
2 fif|ty

3 fif|teen
4 to|mo|rrow
5 Ger|man

CAN YOU understand this text?

Read the profiles and complete the chart for Mark, Bianca, and Jacek. Then add information about you.

 I'm **Mark Davis**. I'm from Seattle in the USA. I'm a teacher. I'm twenty-eight and I'm single.

 I'm **Bianca Costa**. I'm from Rio in Brazil. I'm twenty. I'm single and I'm a student.

 I'm **Jacek Popko**. I'm forty. I'm from Krakow in Poland. I'm married, with two children. I'm a doctor.

First name	Mark	Bianca	Jacek	_____ (= you)
Surname				
Age	28			
Nationality				
Marital status		single		
Occupation			doctor	

▶ CAN YOU understand these people?

◀ **2.28** Watch or listen and answer the questions.

| 1 | 2 | 3 | 4 | 5 |
| — | Vera | Richard | Mairi | Iain |

1 The woman's name is ____.
  a Gayna
  b Jeina
  c Jayna
2 Vera is ____.
  a Mexican
  b Russian
  c Canadian
3 Richard is ____ years old.
  a 46
  b 56
  c 66
4 Mairi's phone number is ____.
  a 07564378
  b 07654378
  c 07563478
5 Iain's email address is ____.
  a iain.smith@yahoo.co.uk
  b iain.6@yahoo.com
  c iain.smith@yahoo.com

CAN YOU say this in English?

Tick (✓) the boxes.

Can you...?	Yes, I can.
1 say your name and where you are from	☐
2 ask where other people are from	☐
3 spell your name	☐
4 count from 0 to 100	☐
5 ask for and give personal information, e.g. name, address, age, etc.	☐
6 say your phone number	☐
7 use and understand classroom language	☐
8 check into a hotel	☐
9 book a table at a restaurant	☐

Is it an ID card?

No, it's a credit card.

1 VOCABULARY small things

a What are the four things? Can you remember?

b **V** p.119 **Vocabulary Bank** Small things

2 GRAMMAR singular and plural nouns, a / an

a Read the list. What do you think are the top four things?

Oh no! Where's my phone?

Every day people all over the world say, 'Oh no! Where's my...?' The top eight things that people look for are (not in the correct order):

- [ ] pens and pencils
- [ ] glasses and sunglasses
- [ ] keys (house keys and car keys)
- [ ] wallets and purses
- [ ] bank cards
- [ ] mobile phones
- [ ] umbrellas
- [ ] phone chargers

Adapted from the British Press

b 🔊 **3.2** Listen and number the things 1–8 in the list in **a**. Is this order true for you?

For me, number one is my glasses.

c Look at the photos. Complete the chart.

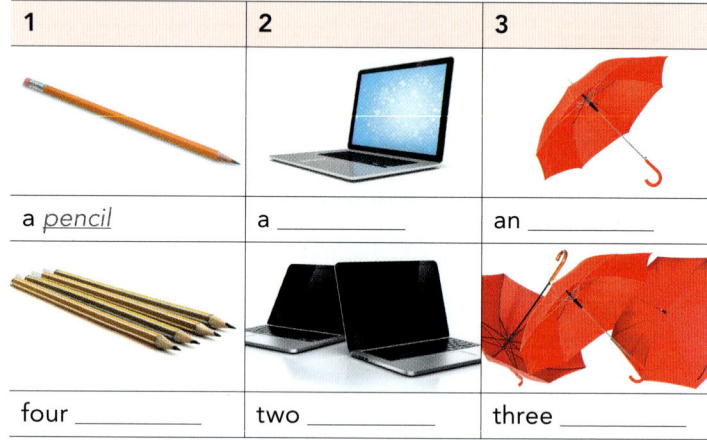

1	2	3
a *pencil*	a _____	an _____
four _____	two _____	three _____

d **G** p.96 **Grammar Bank 3A**

e **C** **Communication** Memory game p.81 Remember the things in the photo.

3 PRONUNCIATION /z/ and /s/, plural endings

a 🔊 **3.5** Listen and repeat the words and sound.

z zebra	zero Brazil is he's

b 🔊 **3.6** Listen and repeat the plural words and sounds.

z	bags phones keys pens
s	books coats passports tablets
/ɪz/	watches glasses pieces purses

c 🔊 **3.7** Listen. Say the plural.

1 🔊 *It's a photo.* *They're photos.*

4 LISTENING

a 🔊 **3.8** Listen to five situations. Number the photos 1–5.

b Listen again. Write the small things for each situation.

1 _____
2 _____
3 _____
4 _____
5 _____

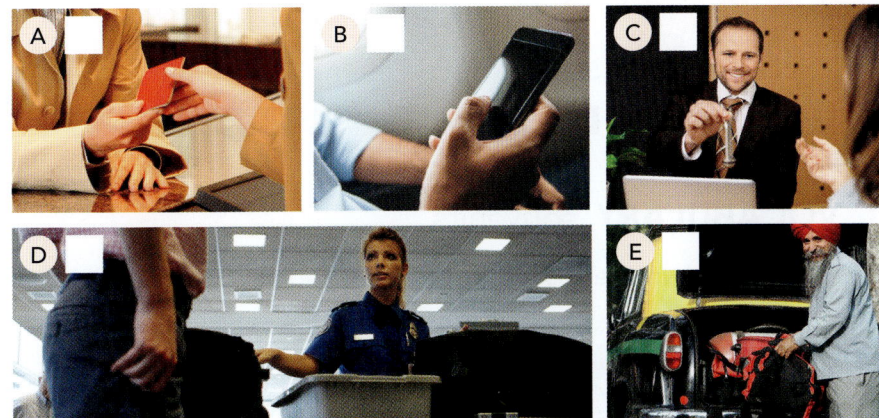

5 SPEAKING

a Look at the photos. What are the things? Work with a partner. **A** ask **B** about photo 1. **B** ask **A** about photo 2. Continue with the other photos.

What is it? *(I think) it's a / an…*

What are they? *(I think) they're…*

I don't know.

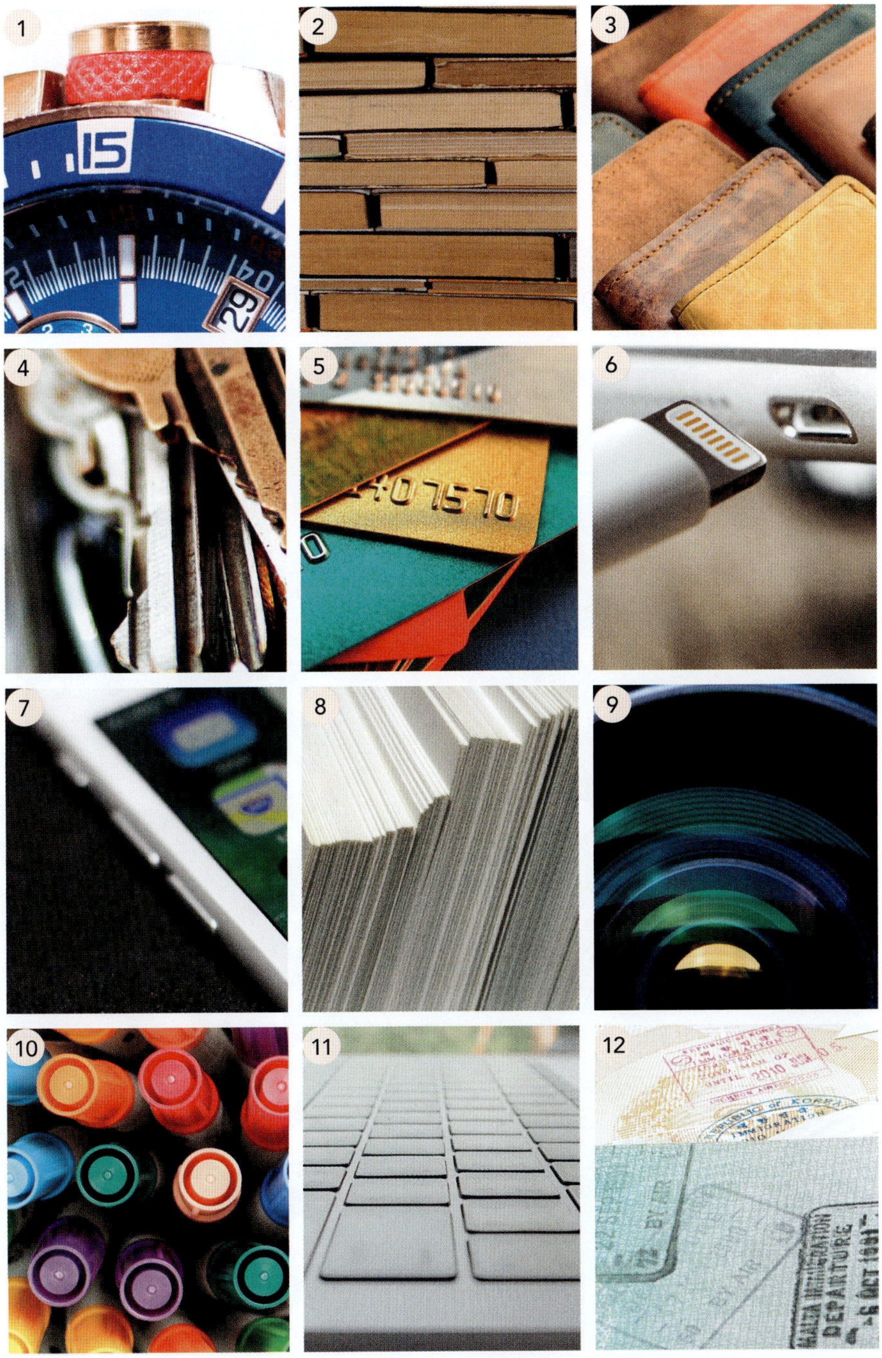

b What's in your bag or pocket? Tick (✓) the things.

☐ a book
☐ a credit card
☐ glasses
☐ an ID card
☐ keys
☐ a pen
☐ a pencil
☐ a phone
☐ a photo
☐ a purse
☐ an umbrella
☐ a wallet

c Now tell a partner.

In my bag, I have a book, keys, a pen…

d What other things do you have in your bag or pocket? Ask your teacher.

What's…in English? How do you spell it?

WORDS AND PHRASES TO LEARN 3A

p.131 Listen and repeat the words and phrases.

3B Souvenirs

What are those? They're key rings.

G *this / that / these / those* **V** souvenirs **P** /ð/, sentence rhythm

1 VOCABULARY souvenirs

a 3.10 Look at the eight things. Listen and repeat the words.

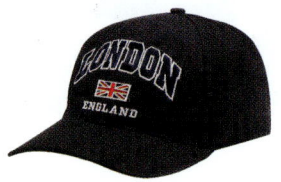

1 a cap /kæp/

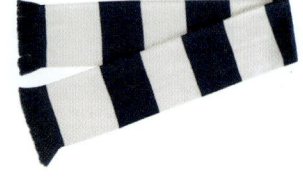

2 a football scarf /ˈfʊtbɔːl skɑːf/

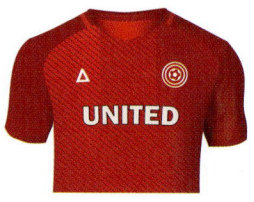

3 a football shirt /ˈfʊtbɔːl ʃɜːt/

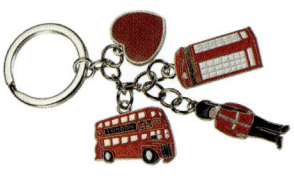

4 a key ring /ˈkiː rɪŋ/

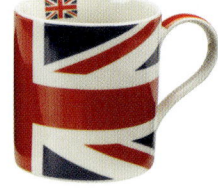

5 a mug /mʌɡ/

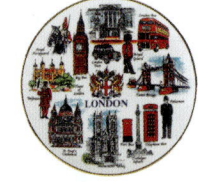

6 a plate /pleɪt/

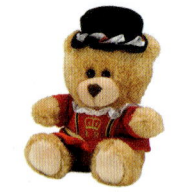

7 a teddy /ˈtedi/

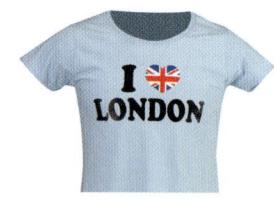

8 a T-shirt /ˈtiː ʃɜːt/

b Cover the words and photos and look at the souvenir stall. Say the souvenirs 1–8.

c What are typical souvenirs in your country?

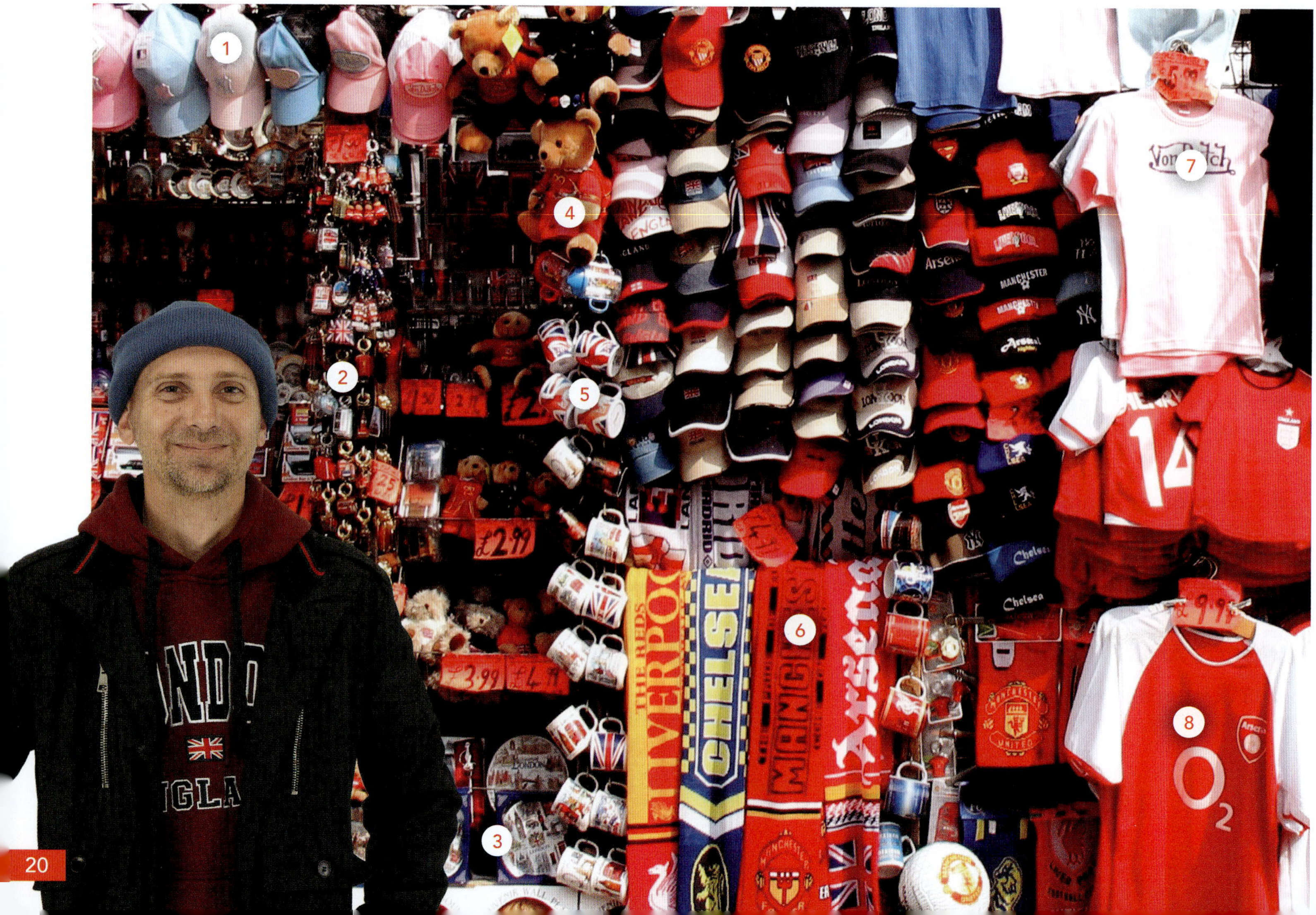

2 LISTENING

a **◉ 3.11** Listen and complete the conversation with numbers.

Woman	Excuse me. What are *those*?
Man	They're T-shirts.
Woman	How much are they?
Man	They're [1] £_____.

Woman	And how much are *these* key rings?
Man	They're [2] £_____.
Woman	And *this* mug?
Man	[3] £_____.

Woman	Is *that* a Manchester United shirt?
Man	No, it's Arsenal.
Woman	How much is it?
Man	[4] £_____.
Woman	Oh…no. Thank you. Bye.

b **◉ 3.12** Listen and repeat the conversation in **a**. Then practise with a partner.

c **◉ 3.13** Listen. What does the woman buy?

3 GRAMMAR *this / that / these / those*

a Read the conversation in **2** again. Complete the chart with the highlighted words.

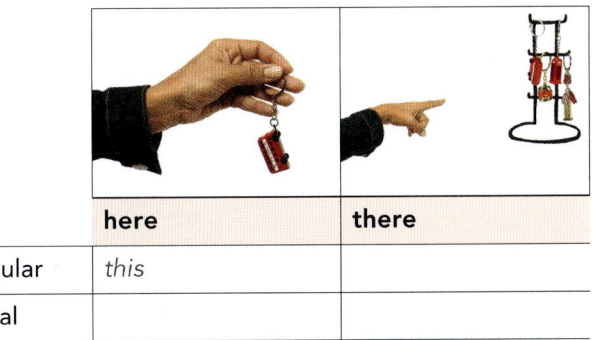

	here	**there**
singular	*this*	
plural		

b **G p.96 Grammar Bank 3B**

4 PRONUNCIATION & SPEAKING
/ð/, sentence rhythm

a **◉ 3.15** Listen and repeat the words and sound.

🔴 mother	this that these those the they	

b **◉ 3.16** Listen and complete the conversations with words and numbers.

1 How much is this _____?
  It's £_____.
2 How much is that _____?
  It's £_____.
3 How much are these _____?
  They're £_____.
4 How much are those _____?
  They're £_____.
5 Two _____, please.
  That's £_____.

c Listen again. Then repeat the conversations. Copy the rhythm.

d **C Communication** How much are these watches?
A p.79 B p.83 Role-play conversations.

WORDS AND PHRASES TO LEARN 3B

p.131 Listen and repeat the words and phrases.

Go online to review the lesson

1 UNDERSTANDING PRICES

a 🔊 **3.18** Listen and repeat.

ten **pounds**   fifty **pence** (fifty **p**)

ten **euros**   fifty **cents**

ten **dollars**   twenty-five **cents**

b Match the prices and words.

1	*H* £12.75	A	thirteen dollars twenty-five
2	€15.99	B	eighty cents
3	$50.19	C	five pounds thirty-five
4	£5.35	D	fifteen euros ninety-nine
5	$13.25	E	sixty pence
6	€3.20	F	fifty dollars nineteen
7	€0.25	G	three euros twenty
8	£1.50	H	~~twelve pounds seventy-five~~
9	60p	I	one pound fifty
10	$0.80	J	twenty-five cents

c 🔊 **3.19** Listen and check. Then listen and repeat.

d Cover the words and look at the prices. Practise saying them.

e 🔊 **3.20** Listen to four conversations. How much is it? Circle the correct price.

1	newspaper:	$2.50	$2.15
2	umbrella:	€15	€50
3	memory card:	$4.99	$9.49
4	train ticket:	£13.20	£30.20

2 PRONUNCIATION /ʊə/, /s/, and /k/

🔊 **3.21** Listen and repeat the words and sounds.

	tourist	euro Europe European
	snake	cent city pence price
	key	coffee camera credit card

> 🔍 **The letter c**
> c = /s/ before e and i, e.g. cent, city.
> c = /k/ before other letters, e.g. coffee.

3 ▶ BUYING LUNCH

a 🔊 **3.22** Read the menu. Then listen and repeat the food, drinks, and prices.

THE THREE KINGS
MENU
FOOD
THREE KINGS BURGER £7.99
PIES (STEAK OR CHICKEN) £9.20
SANDWICHES £4.15
(CHEESE OR TUNA)
SALAD (CHICKEN OR EGG) £5.99
DRINK
MINERAL WATER £1.90
ORANGE JUICE £2.80
COKE/DIET COKE £2.60
£3.25
BEER
COFFEE/TEA £1.95

b Practise with a partner. Ask the prices on the menu.

How much is a tuna sandwich?   *£4.15.*

g 🔊 **3.25** Watch or listen to Jenny and her friend Amy in a New York deli. How much is Jenny's lunch?

c 🔊 **3.23** Watch or listen to Rob in a London pub. Tick (✓) the things he orders on the menu in **a**.

d Watch or listen again and complete the conversation.

Barman	Who's next?
Rob	Can I have a ¹_____ sandwich, please?
Barman	Anything else?
Rob	And a ²_____, please.
Barman	Ice and lemon?
Rob	³_____, thanks.
Barman	There you go.
Rob	Thanks. How much is it?
Barman	⁴_____.
Rob	Here you ⁵_____.
Barman	Thanks. Here's your change.

h Watch or listen again. What do they have? Complete the chart.

Jenny	
Amy	

4 ▶ USEFUL PHRASES

🔊 **3.26** Watch or listen and repeat the useful phrases.

Can I have a cheese sandwich, please?	Here you are.
	Here's your change.
Anything else?	I'm fine, too.
And a Coke, please.	Wait for me.
Ice and lemon?	Sure!
No, thanks.	Great idea.
How much is it?	

e 🔊 **3.24** Watch or listen and repeat. Then practise the conversation with a partner.

f Now role-play the conversation in pairs. **A** You are the barman. **B** Order food and a drink. Then change roles.

🔵 **Go online** to watch the video and review the lesson

4A Meet the family

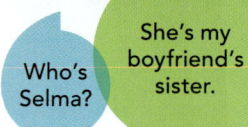

Who's Selma?

She's my boyfriend's sister.

G possessive adjectives, possessive 's **V** people and family **P** /ʌ/, /æ/, and /ə/

1 VOCABULARY people and family

a Look at the photos. Match the words to people 1–4.

| a boy | a girl | a man | a woman |

b 🔊 4.1 Listen and check.

c **V** p.120 **Vocabulary Bank** People and family

2 PRONUNCIATION /ʌ/, /æ/, and /ə/

a 🔊 4.5 Listen and repeat the words and sounds.

⬆ up	husband Sunday son mother brother
🐱 cat	man family bag thanks that
💻 computer	mother sister daughter children woman

> 🔍 /ə/
> /ə/ is a very common vowel sound in syllables that aren't stressed, e.g. final -er = /ə/ (mother, daughter, etc.).

b 🔊 4.6 Listen and repeat. Practise the sentences.
'Is Justin your husband?' 'No, he's my brother.'
I have a big family. That's my grandfather.
The woman over there is my sister.

3 GRAMMAR possessive adjectives, possessive 's

a 🔊 4.7 Read and listen to the conversation on p.25. Do you think Sarah is a) a friend of the family b) a new babysitter?

b Look at photo A. Point to the people and say their names.

(He's Mark.

c Read and listen again. Then complete the chart with a highlighted phrase.

I	my husband
you	
he	
she	
it	
we	our children
you (plural)	
they	

d Read Part B again. Complete the sentences.
1 The name of the restaurant is _____ Bistro.
2 My _____ phone number is there, too.

e 🔊 4.8 Listen. Do you think Sarah is a good babysitter?

f **G** p.98 **Grammar Bank 4A**

g Point to people in the classroom. What are their names?

(What's his name?
   (What's her name?

h Look at photo A on p.25. With a partner, say as much as you can about each person.

(His name's Oliver. He's Maria's son / Emma's brother.

A

Maria	Hi, Sarah! Come in.
Sarah	Thanks.
Maria	This is my husband, Mark.
Mark	Hello.
Sarah	Hi.
Maria	And these are our children.
Children	Hello!
Sarah	What are their names?
Maria	Her name's Emma, and his name's Oliver.
Emma	And this is our cat.
Sarah	Ah! What's its name?
Emma	*Her* name is Princess. She's a girl.
Sarah	Oh, sorry.

B

Maria	The name of the restaurant is Mario's Bistro. The phone number's on the table over there.
Sarah	Great, thanks.
Maria	And my husband's phone number is there, too.
Sarah	OK. And your number is in my phone.
Maria	Now, children. Sarah is your babysitter. Be good.
Children	OK, Mum.

4 LISTENING

a 🔊 **4.11** Jane is in Italy with her friend Marina. It's her birthday. Look at her birthday card and listen. Who are the people?

1 Paul is *Jane*'s *brother*.
2 Hayley is _____'s _____.
3 Susan is _____'s _____.
4 Nicole is _____'s _____.
5 John is _____'s _____.

b Listen again. Answer the questions.

1 How old are Paul and Nicole?
2 Who are Sally and Max?

5 SPEAKING & WRITING

a Work with a partner:

A and **B** write the names of six people (your family or friends) on a piece of paper.

A give your piece of paper to **B**. **B** give your piece of paper to **A**.

A ask **B** about his / her people. **B** ask **A** about his / her people.

Who's Marco? (*He's my sister's husband.*

b **W** p.86 **Writing** A post about a photo
Write about a photo of your family.

WORDS AND PHRASES TO LEARN 4A

p.131 Listen and repeat the words and phrases.

Go online to review the lesson

G adjectives   V colours and common adjectives   P /ɑː/ and /ɔː/, linking

Is it a good car?

No, it isn't. It's small and very slow.

1 LISTENING & VOCABULARY
colours and common adjectives

a Do the quiz with a partner. Match the logos to the cars. What nationality are they?

1 is a Jaguar. I think it's English. Or American.

CAR QUIZ

1
2
3
4
5
6

Chevrolet
Honda   Ferrari
Mercedes   Peugeot   Jaguar

b 4.13 Listen and check.

c 4.14 Now look at the picture and listen to the conversation. Which car is perfect for the woman...?

  a in her opinion   b in her son's opinion

d Read the conversation. Write the highlighted words under the two cars.

Salesman	Is the car for you, sir?
Man	No, it's for my mother.
Woman	Yes, it's for me.
Salesman	For you, madam? Well, what about this blue car here? It's small and it's easy to park.
Man	Yes, Mum, it's perfect for you.
Woman	But it's very slow. And it's ugly.
Salesman	It's an electric car, madam. Very eco-friendly. They're good cars.
Woman	I prefer...this red car.
Man	But Mum, it's a sports car! It's very fast. And it's very expensive.
Woman	Yes, but it's my money. It's a beautiful car and I love it! How much is it?
Salesman	Come with me, madam.
Man	Mum! ...

e 4.15 Listen and repeat the conversation. Then practise it in groups of three.

f V p.121 Vocabulary Bank Adjectives

g With a partner, talk about your car or your family's car.

My car is a Peugeot 208. It's French. It's small and it's green. It isn't very fast.

2 GRAMMAR adjectives

a (Circle) a or b.

1 a It's a beautiful car.
  b It's a car beautiful.
2 a They're goods cars.
  b They're good cars.

b **G** p.98 Grammar Bank 4B

c ◀) 4.20 Listen and say the plural.

1 ◀) *an American car* (*American cars*

3 PRONUNCIATION /ɑː/ and /ɔː/, linking

a ◀) 4.21 Listen and repeat the words and sounds.

car	fast father park garden are
horse	short sport small awful

b ◀) 4.22 Listen. Practise the phrases.

a big umbrella   an old man
a short email   an orange coat
brown eggs   an expensive watch

c ◀) 4.23 Listen and write five phrases.

d With a partner, look at the photos from **Vocabulary Bank** Adjectives and make sentences.

(*It's a black bag.* (*They're blue keys.*

4 SPEAKING

Talk in small groups.

I prefer small cities.) (*Me too.* (*I prefer big cities.*

big small
cities

Japanese Mexican
food

British American
films

cheap expensive
restaurants

old new
houses

long short
books

big small
dogs

black and white colour
photos

5 ▶ VIDEO LISTENING Beaulieu Motor Museum

a Watch the video *Beaulieu Motor Museum*. Which is your favourite car?

b Watch again. Mark the sentences **T** (true) or **F** (false).

1 Beaulieu is a small village.
2 It isn't famous.
3 The National Motor Museum is 52 years old.
4 The presenter's favourite car is the Bluebird.
5 The Ferrari Dino is 14 years old.
6 The Ford Anglia is an American car.
7 It's famous because it's in the Star Wars films.
8 The National Motor Museum has motorbikes, too.

c Do you think it's an interesting museum?

WORDS AND PHRASES TO LEARN 4B

p.131 Listen and repeat the words and phrases.

(**Go online** to watch the video and review the lesson

GRAMMAR

Circle a or b.

_____'s your name?
a Who   b What

1 Look! It's _____ email from Melanie.
a an   b a

2 A Where are my sunglasses?   B _____ in your bag.
a It's   b They're

3 These are Swiss _____.
a watchs   b watches

4 Kyoto and Osaka are two important _____ in Japan.
a citys   b cities

5 A What's _____?
B It's a key ring.
a this   b these

6 How much are _____ T-shirts?
a those   b that

7 Look at _____ house over there. It's beautiful.
a this   b that

8 _____ my friend, Tom.
a It is   b This is

9 He's Swiss. _____ name is Ken.
a His   b Her

10 We're Mr and Mrs Brown. _____ son is in class 4.
a Our   b Their

11 Justin is _____ brother.
a Sophies   b Sophie's

12 My _____ is Amanda.
a name's wife   b wife's name

13 These chairs are _____.
a very expensive   b very expensives

14 A Ferrari is a _____.
a car fast   b fast car

15 They're _____.
a good photos   b goods photos

VOCABULARY

a Write a / an + the things.

a wallet   1 _____   2 _____

3 _____   4 _____   5 _____

---

b Complete the chart.

	man	father	2 _____	son	4 _____	boyfriend
	woman	1 _____	wife	3 _____	sister	5 _____

c Write the plural.

mother + father = parents

1 a woman   two _____
2 a child   three _____
3 a man   four _____
4 a person   50 _____

d Write the colours.

☐ white

1 ■ _____   4 ■ _____
2 ■ _____   5 ■ _____
3 ■ _____   6 ■ _____

e Write the opposite adjectives.

fast slow   3 long _____
1 big _____   4 new _____
2 expensive _____   5 ugly _____

PRONUNCIATION

a Write the words for the sound pictures.

_____   _____
bike   3

_____   _____
1   4

_____   _____
2   5

b  p.134–5 Sound Bank Look at more words with the sounds in a, and these sounds:

Practise saying the example words.

c Underline the stressed syllable.

um|bre|lla   2 fa|mi|ly   4 ex|pen|sive
1 wo|man   3 o|range   5 sis|ter

CAN YOU understand this text?

a Read the two texts and write the people's names in the pictures.

1 _____ 3 _____
2 _____ 4 _____

My name's Jeremy Fisher and I'm from Liverpool, in the UK. I'm married to Anna and I have two children, a son and a daughter. My son's name is Matthew. He's 17. He's tall with dark hair. My daughter's name is Susanna. She's 19. I think my children are good-looking, probably because their mother is beautiful!

1 _____ 2 _____ 3 _____

My name's Claire and I'm from Nantes in France. I'm 22. I have two sisters. Their names are Anne and Louise. Anne is 24. She's good-looking, with long blond hair. She isn't married. Louise is 31 and very different from Anne, but she's good-looking too. She's married. Her husband's name is Marius.

b Read again and answer the questions with a sentence.

1 What's Jeremy's surname?
_____

2 Where is he from?
_____

3 What's his son's name?
_____

4 How old is Susanna?
_____

5 What nationality is Claire?
_____

6 Who is Anne?
_____

7 Is she married?
_____

8 How old is Louise?
_____

▶ CAN YOU understand these people?

◀)) 4.25 Watch or listen and answer the questions.

1 Richard 2 Rachel 3 Kieran 4 Debra 5 Susan

1 What's in Richard's bag?
   a his keys
   b his coat
   c his camera
2 What's in Rachel's bag?
   a her phone, pencils and charger
   b her notebook, purse and passport
   c her phone, purse and umbrella
3 There are ____ people in Kieran's family.
   a 4
   b 5
   c 6
4 A cup of coffee in Debra's local coffee shop is ____.
   a cheap
   b £4
   c $4
5 Susan's car is ____.
   a big
   b green
   c a Fiat

CAN YOU say this in English?

Tick (✓) the boxes.

Can you...?	Yes, I can.
1 say what's in your bag	▢
2 talk about things with *this*, *that*, *these*, and *those*	▢
3 say who is in your family	▢
4 introduce somebody	▢
5 describe cars	▢
6 ask for things in a café or store	▢
7 ask about prices	▢

Go online to watch the video, review Files 3 & 4, and check your progress

G present simple ⊞ and ⊟ : *I, you, we, they*   **V** food and drink   **P** /dʒ/ and /g/

> We have fruit and cereal for breakfast.

> I don't have breakfast. I have a coffee at work.

1 VOCABULARY food and drink

a Re-order the letters to make food and drink words. Match them to photos A–E.

1 ☐ AET
_____

2 ☐ ESHECE
_____

3 ☐ GRANEO CUJIE
_____

4 ☐ WANDCHIS
_____

5 ☐ GESG
_____

b 🔊 5.1 Listen and check.

c Ⓥ p.122 **Vocabulary Bank** Food and drink

2 READING & SPEAKING

a Look at the photos and read the article and comments. Who thinks breakfast is a) important, b) not important?

b 🔊 5.4 Complete the comments with food and drink words. Then listen and check.

c Read the comments again. Ⓒircle the places where they have breakfast. Underline the other words for food and drink.

d Is breakfast important for you? What do you have? Where do you have it?

A good breakfast – is it important?

Is breakfast a very important meal, or not important at all?
Scientists and doctors have different opinions: some think that a big breakfast is good for you, because you eat less during the day; others say that if you aren't hungry, don't have breakfast – it's only extra calories!

Is breakfast important for *you*? Send us a photo of your breakfast.

Comments

Marta, Italy
I have breakfast in a great café near my office. I have a ¹**cr**_oissant_ and coffee – an espresso with hot ²**m**_____. Mmmm. I love breakfast! It's my favourite meal.

Paulo, Brazil
I have breakfast at home, but I don't have a big breakfast. I have ³**fr**_____ and ⁴**y**_____, and sometimes toast. It's a healthy breakfast. That's a good thing at the beginning of the day.

Rob, UK
I don't eat in the morning – I'm not hungry. I just have a ⁵**c**_____ at work. But I have lunch early, at about 12.30.

Sakura, Japan
I really like breakfast. It's an important meal for Japanese people. I have breakfast at home with my family. We have a traditional breakfast. It isn't very different from lunch and dinner. We have ⁶**r**_____, ⁷**f**_____, and miso soup and we drink green tea. We don't drink a lot of coffee in my family.

3 GRAMMAR present simple ⊞ and ⊟: I, you, we, they

a Complete the sentences from the comments in **2**.

present simple ⊞ and ⊟	
⊞	**Marta**
	1 I _____ breakfast in a great café.
	Sakura
	2 I really _____ breakfast.
	3 We _____ a traditional breakfast.
⊟	**Paulo**
	4 I _____ _____ a big breakfast.
	Rob
	5 I _____ _____ in the morning.
	Sakura
	6 We _____ _____ a lot of coffee in my family.

b 🄖 p.100 **Grammar Bank 5A**

c Look at **Vocabulary Bank** Food and drink **p.122** Say what you like 🙂 and don't like 🙁.

(I like fish. I don't like meat.

4 LISTENING

a 🔊 5.6 Listen to Anna talk about her favourite meal. Complete her column in the chart.

	Anna	Will	Sarah
Favourite meal	dinner	lunch	breakfast
Where?	¹ At _____ or at a _____.	⁴ At _____.	⁷ Usually at _____. On Wednesdays at a _____.
Food	² _____ or _____ and _____.	⁵ Different things but with _____.	⁸ _____ and an _____. On Wednesdays a _____.
Drink	³ A glass of _____.	⁶ _____ and then a _____.	⁹ _____ or _____. On Wednesdays _____.

b 🔊 5.7 Now repeat for Will and Sarah.

c What's *your* favourite meal of the day?

5 PRONUNCIATION /dʒ/ and /g/

a 🔊 5.8 Listen and repeat the words and sounds.

dʒ	**jazz**	juice vegetables orange
g	**girl**	sugar yogurt eggs

🔍 **g and j**
Remember *j* always = /dʒ/. *g* is sometimes /g/ (e.g. *sugar*) and sometimes /dʒ/ (e.g. *orange*), especially before *e*.

b 🔊 5.9 Listen. Practise the sentences.
I'm Jane. I like orange juice and vegetables.
I'm Grace. I have eggs, and coffee with sugar.

6 SPEAKING

a Complete the sentences so they are true about **you** and people in your country.

Food: you and your country
You
I have breakfast _____. (Where?)
I have _____ for breakfast. (What?)
I have lunch _____. (Where?)
I have dinner with _____. (Who?)
I eat a lot of _____. (What?)
I love _____. (What?)
I don't like _____. (What?)
Your country
People have _____ for breakfast. (What?)
They have a big _____. (lunch / dinner)
They _____ a lot of food from other countries. (eat / don't eat)
They eat a lot of _____. (What?)
They drink a lot of _____. (What?)

b Talk to a partner. Say your first sentence. Then say *What about you?*

I have breakfast at home. What about you?)

(I have breakfast at home, too.

7 WRITING

Ⓦ p.86 **Writing** A comment post Write about your breakfast.

WORDS AND PHRASES TO LEARN 5A

p.131 Listen and repeat the words and phrases.

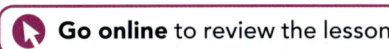 🄖 **Go online** to review the lesson

G present simple ?: *I, you, we, they* **V** common verb phrases 1 **P** /w/ and /v/, sentence rhythm and linking

Do you live in New York?

No, I don't. I live in London.

1 GRAMMAR present simple ?: *I, you, we, they*

a 🔊 5.11 Eve, a British woman, and Wendy, an American woman, are on a flight from London to New York. Listen to the conversation and number the pictures 1–4.

1	Eve	Do you like the ¹_____?
	Wendy	Yes, I do. It's very good.
	Eve	She's my favourite writer. I love her books.

2	Eve	Do you live in ²_____?
	Wendy	No, I don't. I live in London. My husband and I work for a British company.
	Eve	Oh! Do you have ³_____?
	Wendy	No, we don't.
	Eve	I have two sons and a daughter. David and Andrew are at university and Carla's at school. Look. Here are some photos… This is a photo of our holiday in Barbados. Do you know Barbados?
	Wendy	No, I don't.

3	Attendant	Do you want ⁴_____, fish, or pasta?
	Eve	Oh, fish, please.
	Wendy	Pasta for me, please.
	Eve	How's your pasta?
	Wendy	It's OK.
	Eve	This fish isn't very good. Excuse me, I don't like this fish. Can I have the ⁵_____, please?
	Attendant	I'm sorry, madam. It's finished.

4	Eve	Oh, I need to go to the toilet. Oops, sorry.
	Wendy	Excuse me. What ⁶_____ do we arrive?
	Attendant	In 25 minutes, madam.
	Wendy	That's good!

b Read the conversation and complete it with words from the list.

book   children   meat   New York   pasta   time

c Listen again and check.

d Underline the questions and short answers in parts 1 and 2 of the conversation.

e 🅖 p.100 **Grammar Bank 5B**

A

B

C

D

2 VOCABULARY common verb phrases 1

a Match the phrases.

1 I love   d   a in London.
2 I live   b two sons and a daughter.
3 I work   c for a British company.
4 I want   d her books.
5 I have   e the fish, please.

b Ⓥ p.123 **Vocabulary Bank** Common verb phrases 1

c Write four true sentences about <u>you</u>, two positive and two negative.

I watch the BBC.   I don't read a newspaper.

d In pairs, read your sentences to each other. Are any of them the same?

3 LISTENING

a 🔊 5.15 At the end of her holiday, Eve gets a taxi back to the airport. Read sentences 1–10 and look at the **bold** words. Then listen and (circle) a or b.

1 a Her flight is from **Newark** airport.
   (b) Her flight is from **JFK**.
2 a The traffic is **bad**.
   b The traffic is **good**.
3 a Eve is from **Manchester**.
   b Eve is from **London**.
4 a The taxi driver is from **New York**.
   b The taxi driver is from **Puerto Rico**.
5 a London is very **cheap**.
   b London is very **expensive**.
6 a The taxi driver has two **sons**.
   b The taxi driver has two **daughters**.
7 a The taxi is **$87.50**.
   b The taxi is **$87.15**.
8 a The taxi driver says 'Have a good **day**.'
   b The taxi driver says 'Have a good **flight**.'
9 a Eve **is late**.
   b Eve **isn't late**.
10 a The gate number is **B5**.
   b The gate number is **C5**.

b 🔊 5.16 Listen to what happens in the airport. Why does Eve say 'What a nice surprise!'?

4 PRONUNCIATION & SPEAKING
/w/ and /v/, sentence rhythm and linking

a 🔊 5.17 Listen and repeat the words and sounds.

w	**w**itch	**w**ant **w**ork **wh**en **wh**ere
v	**v**ase	**v**ery ha**v**e li**v**e TV

b 🔊 5.18 Listen. Notice the linked (‿) words.

1 A Do you **live** in a **flat**?
   B **No**, I **don't**. I **live** in a **house**.

2 A Do you **have** a big **family**?
   B **Yes**, I **do**. I **have** three **sisters**.

3 A Do you **watch** a lot of **TV**?
   B **No**, I **don't**. I **read books**.

c Listen again and repeat. <u>Copy</u> the <u>rhythm</u>.

d 🔊 5.19 Now listen and write five sentences.

e Complete 2–10 with a verb from the list.

drink eat go have listen ~~live~~
need read speak watch

Do you...

1 *live* near here? / in a house or a flat?
2 _____ brothers and sisters? / a cat or a dog?
3 _____ TV on your phone? / YouTube videos?
4 _____ to pop music? / to classical music?
5 _____ a newspaper? / magazines?
6 _____ meat? / a lot of chocolate?
7 _____ Coke? / beer?
8 _____ French? / German?
9 _____ a new phone? / a new car?
10 _____ to a gym? / to the cinema at weekends?

f Ask and answer questions with a partner.

Do you live near here? *Yes, I do. I live very near.*

Do you live in a house or a flat? *I live in a small flat.*

WORDS AND PHRASES TO LEARN 5B

p.131 Listen and repeat the words and phrases.

Go online to review the lesson

Practical English What time is it?

telling the time **V** the time, saying how you feel **P** /ɒ/, silent consonants

1 ▶ TELLING THE TIME

a ◀)) 5.21 Watch or listen and match the conversations to photos A–C.

A ☐

B ☐

C ☐

1	Rob	I'm tired. What time is it?
	Alan	It's eleven o'clock.
	Rob	I need to go. I have a meeting in Oxford tomorrow morning.
	Alan	One more drink?
	Rob	Oh, OK!
2	Rob	Excuse me. What time is it?
	Woman	It's a quarter to eight. What time's your train?
	Rob	At seven forty-seven.
	Woman	You need to hurry! You only have two minutes.
	Rob	Thanks!
3	Rob	Hello. I'm Rob Walker. I'm sorry I'm late.
	Man	You're an hour late. It's half past ten.
	Rob	I know. I'm really sorry.

b ◀)) 5.22 Watch or listen and repeat the conversations in **a**. Then practise them with a partner.

c Cover the conversations and look at the clocks in photos A–C. What time is it?

2 VOCABULARY the time

a ◀)) 5.23 Listen and repeat the times.

It's three o'clock.   It's five past three.   It's ten past three.

It's (a) quarter past three.   It's twenty past three.   It's twenty-five past three.

It's half past three.   It's twenty-five to four.   It's twenty to four.

It's (a) quarter to four.   It's ten to four.   It's five to four.

b Cover the times. Look at the clocks and say the times.

c ◀)) 5.24 Listen and draw the times on the clocks.

 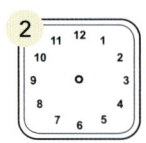 

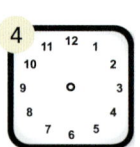  

> 🔎 **The time**
> 1 You can also say the time with numbers, e.g.
>   7.15 = (a) quarter past seven **OR** seven fifteen.
> 2 60 minutes /ˈmɪnɪts/ = one hour /aʊə/.

d Practise with a partner.

Number 1. What time is it?) (*It's twenty to nine.*

e 🟢 **Communication** What time is it? **A** p.79 **B** p.83 Ask and answer about times.

3 PRONUNCIATION /ɒ/, silent consonants

a 5.25 Listen and repeat the words and sound.

clock	what Oxford sorry coffee

b 🔊 5.26 Listen and repeat the words. Practise saying them.

eig̶ht hal̶f h̶our k̶now listen tir̶ed tw̶o
Wed̶nesday wha̶t w̶rite

> 🔍 **Silent letters**
> Some English words have a 'silent letter', e.g. in *where*, you don't pronounce the *h* /weə/.

c 🔊 5.27 Listen to the conversations. Then practise with a partner.

> A What time is it?
> B It's half past two.
>
> A Is the meeting on Wednesday?
> B I don't know.
>
> A Listen and write five sentences.
> B Oh no! I'm tired.

4 VOCABULARY saying how you feel

a 🔊 5.28 Listen and repeat the sentences.

1 I'm tired.   2 I'm cold.   3 I'm <u>hun</u>gry.

4 I'm hot.   5 I'm <u>thir</u>sty.

b Match the sentences in **a** to a–e.

a ☐ Time for lunch.
b ☐ Time for bed.
c ☐ It's 5° (degrees /dɪˈɡriːz/) this morning.
d ☐ I need a glass of water.
e ☐ It's 35°!

c 🔊 5.29 Listen and check. How do <u>you</u> feel at the moment?

5 ▶ A NIGHT OUT

a 🔊 5.30 Watch or listen to Jenny and Amy. Tick (✓) the two places they go to.

☐ a bar
☐ a café
☐ a theatre
☐ a cinema
☐ a restaurant

b Watch or listen again. Complete sentences 1–3 with times.

1 The show is at _____.
2 Jenny and Amy meet at _____.
3 The show ends at _____.

6 ▶ USEFUL PHRASES

🔊 5.31 Watch or listen and repeat the useful phrases.

I need to go.	What a great show!
You need to hurry.	It's late and I'm tired.
You're an hour late.	Come on.
I'm really sorry.	OK. Let's go.
Don't worry.	

> 🖱 **Go online** to watch the video and review the lesson

6A A school reunion

She's a journalist. She works for a newspaper.

What does she do?

1 VOCABULARY jobs and places of work

a Look at the photos. What are their jobs?

1 He's a **t**_____ dr_____.
2 She's a **t**_____.
3 He's a **r**_____.

b **V** p.124 **Vocabulary Bank** Jobs and places of work

c Choose a job from **Vocabulary Bank** Jobs and places of work. Ask five other students the questions. Answer their questions.

(*What do you do?* (*Where do you work?*

2 GRAMMAR present simple: *he, she, it*

a Look at the picture. Why are the people together?

b **6.4** Cover the conversation and listen. Mark the sentences **T** (true) or **F** (false).

1 Anna is a journalist.
2 She works for a magazine.
3 Matt is a teacher.
4 He teaches English.
5 Laura is Matt's daughter.

c Listen again and read the conversation. Check your answers.

d Read the conversation again and complete the chart.

present simple, third person	
I / you	he / she
+ **I work** for a newspaper.	**She** _____ for a newspaper.
– **I don't wear** glasses.	**She** _____ glasses.
? What **do you** do?	What _____ **he** do?

e **G** p.102 **Grammar Bank 6A**

Julia	Who's that over there?
Sarah	It's Anna, you know, the intelligent girl.
Julia	She's very different! Her hair's blonde.
Sarah	Yes, and she doesn't wear glasses now.
Julia	What does she do?
Sarah	She's a journalist. She works for a newspaper – *The Times*, I think.
Julia	Is she good?
Sarah	I don't know. I don't read *The Times*.

Julia	And who's that man with grey hair? Is it Matt?
Sarah	Yes!
Julia	What does he do?
Sarah	He's a teacher. He teaches French.
Julia	Where does he work?
Sarah	At our old school!
Julia	No! At our old school?
Sarah	Yes, and he's married to Laura!
Julia	Laura? From our class? How awful! Is she here?
Sarah	Yes, she's with Matt.
Julia	Very ugly shoes.
Sarah	Yes, horrible.

Laura	Sarah, Julia, hi! Great to see you!
Julia	Hi, Laura. Wow, I *love* your shoes – they're beautiful…

3 PRONUNCIATION third person -es

a 🔊6.6 Listen and (circle) the words where final -es = /ɪz/.

does finishes goes likes lives teaches watches writes

b 🔊6.7 Listen. Change the sentences. Use the third person.

1)) *I live in New York. He…* (*He lives in New York.*

4 READING

a In what jobs in <u>your</u> country do people need to speak English?

b Read the article. Complete 1 and 2 with a job from **Vocabulary Bank** Jobs and places of work p.124.

Do you speak **English** at work?

What do these people have in common? A banker in Mexico City, a barman in a five-star hotel in Moscow, and a worker in the Hitachi electronics factory in Tokyo. They all speak English at work. Do you speak English at work? **Write and tell us.**

1 **Antonio** I work in a restaurant in Madrid. I'm a _____. I speak English at work every day, because a lot of tourists come here. I help customers with the menu and I say what the special dishes are. They are very happy because they can talk to me in English. A lot of tourists don't speak Spanish, but they usually speak English.

2 **Charlotte** I'm a _____ and I work in an office in Paris. It's a multinational company. When people from other countries visit the company, I need to welcome them in English. I also need to answer the phone in English. When we have meetings, we all speak in English, because it's the language of the company.

c 🔊6.8 Now read again and listen. Check your answers.

d Answer the questions with a partner.

1 Why does Antonio speak English at work?
2 How does he help people?
3 Who does Charlotte work for?
4 What two things does she do in English?
5 Why do they speak English in meetings in her company?

> 🔍 *Why…? Because…*
> We use *Why…?* /waɪ/ to ask for a reason, and *Because…* /bɪˈkɒz/ to give a reason.
> **Why** are the tourists happy? **Because** they can talk to Antonio in English.

5 PRONUNCIATION & SPEAKING sentence rhythm

a 🔊6.9 Listen to the conversation.

A **What** does he **do**?
B He's a **nurse**.
A **Where** does he **work**?
B He **works** in a <u>hospital</u>.
A Does he **speak** <u>En</u>glish at **work**?
B **No**, he <u>doesn't</u>.
A Does he **like** his **job**?
B **Yes**, he **does**.

b 🔊6.10 Listen again and repeat. <u>Copy</u> the <u>rhythm</u>.

c Think of two people you know who have jobs. Ask and answer with a partner.

What / he (she) do?
Where / he (she) work?
/ he (she) speak English at work?
/ he (she) like his (her) job? Why?

Person number one is my mother.)
(*What does she do?*

6 WRITING

Write paragraphs about the two people in **5c**.

My mother is a teacher. She works at a primary school in São Paulo. She doesn't speak English at work. She loves her job because she likes children!

WORDS AND PHRASES TO LEARN 6A

p.131 Listen and repeat the words and phrases.

🔄 **Go online** to review the lesson

| What time do you usually get up? | I get up at 7.00. |

G adverbs of frequency   V a typical day   P /j/ and /juː/, sentence rhythm

1 LISTENING & SPEAKING

a Read the questions in **Are you a morning person?** and think about your answers.

b 🔊 6.12 Look at the photos and listen to Hannah answer the questions in **a**. Does she like mornings?

Hannah works for the BBC. Her son, Kit, is three years old.

avocado   bath

c Listen again and write her answers to questions 1–8.

d 🔊 6.13 Listen and repeat questions 1–8.

e Ask your partner the questions. Is he or she a 'morning person'? Why (not)?

2 VOCABULARY a typical day

a Ⓥ p.125 **Vocabulary Bank** A typical day

b Can you remember? Mime or draw five verb phrases for your partner to guess.

Are you a *morning* person?

1 What time do you usually get up?

2 Do you usually feel tired?

3 Do you have a shower or a bath in the morning?

4 Do you always have breakfast? Where?

5 What do you have for breakfast?

6 What time do you go to work (school / university)?

7 Do you usually need to hurry in the morning?

8 Do you like mornings? Why (not)?

3 GRAMMAR adverbs of frequency

a Match sentences 1–4 to a–d.

		M	Tu	W	Th	F
1	I **always** get up at 8.00, … c	✓	✓	✓	✓	✓
2	I **never** drink coffee, …	✗	✗	✗	✗	✗
3	I **usually** finish work at 6.00, …	✓	✓	✓	✓	✗
4	I **sometimes** watch TV, …	✗	✓	✗	✗	✓

a but on Fridays I finish at 3.00.
b or I read and listen to music.
c because I start work at 9.00.
d because I don't like it.

b Ⓖ p.102 **Grammar Bank 6B**

4 PRONUNCIATION /j/ and /juː/, sentence rhythm

a ◉6.17 Listen and repeat the words and sounds.

🛥️	yacht	yes you young yellow
/juː/		usually student music beautiful

b ◉6.18 Listen and repeat. Copy the rhythm.

> **What time** do you **usually have lunch**?
> At **half past one**.
> **What time** do you **usually have dinner**?
> At about **eight o'clock**.
> **What time** do you **usually go** to **bed**?
> At **half past eleven**.

c Ask and answer the questions with a partner.

d In pairs, make true sentences about you. Use *always*, *usually*, *sometimes*, or *never*.

- listen to the radio in the car
- read a newspaper in the morning
- speak English outside class
- watch TV in the evening
- have a big lunch
- do housework at the weekend
- eat fast food
- drink espresso

> *I always listen to the radio in the car. I listen to Radio 2.*

5 SPEAKING & WRITING

a Use the pictures in **Vocabulary Bank A typical day p.125** to tell your partner about your typical evening. Use adverbs of frequency.

> *I never make dinner. My father makes it. We usually have dinner at half past eight.*

b Write about your typical morning and afternoon. Use adverbs of frequency (*always*, *usually*, etc.) and time words (*then*, *after breakfast*, etc.).

6 ▶ VIDEO LISTENING A day in the life of a New York tour guide

a Look at photos A–F from the video *A day in the life of a New York tour guide*. With a partner, number the photos 1–6.

b Watch the video and check your order.

> 🔍 **Glossary**
>
> | US English | British English |
> |---|---|
> | an apartment | a flat |
> | the subway | the Underground |

c Watch again. Mark the sentences **T** (true) or **F** (false).

1 Peter lives in an apartment in Brooklyn.
2 He gets up at seven o'clock.
3 He usually has an omelette for breakfast.
4 He works for a company called Real World Tours.
5 His tours begin at eleven o'clock.
6 He usually has a sandwich for lunch.
7 The tour ends in Wall Street.
8 Peter goes home by subway.
9 In the evening he reads or watches TV.
10 Every day he walks about ten miles.

d Watch some extracts from the video. Complete the sentences with a 'time' word or phrase.

1 _____ _____ he goes there by subway.
2 _____ work, Peter takes the subway back to Brooklyn.
3 _____ he relaxes.

e Do you think Peter's job is easy or difficult? Why?

WORDS AND PHRASES TO LEARN 6B

p.131 Listen and repeat the words and phrases.

▶ **Go online** to watch the video and review the lesson

GRAMMAR

Circle a or b.

_____ 's your name?
a Who   b **What**

1 In Japan, we _____ rice for breakfast.
a have   b has

2 They _____ meat.
a don't eat   b not eat

3 You _____ a lot of fast food. It isn't good for you.
a eats   b eat

4 I _____ tea, I prefer coffee.
a don't drink   b 'm not drink

5 _____ you want a Coke?
a Are   b Do

6 A Do they live near here?
B Yes, they _____.
a do   b live

7 _____ Mexican food?
a Like you   b Do you like

8 A What time _____?
B At 5.30.
a do we arrive   b we arrive

9 _____ she speak Spanish?
a Do   b Does

10 He _____ for a fashion magazine.
a works   b work

11 My brother _____ children.
a don't have   b doesn't have

12 She _____ to the gym after work.
a gos   b goes

13 He _____ a shower before breakfast.
a always has   b has always

14 I _____ to bed before 12.00.
a don't never go   b never go

15 What time _____ lunch?
a you have usually   b do you usually have

VOCABULARY

a Write the words.

bread   1 _____   2 _____

3 _____   4 _____   5 _____

b Complete the verbs.

h_ave_ a shower

1 **r**_____ the newspaper
2 **l**_____ to the radio
3 **g**_____ shopping
4 **l**_____ in a flat
5 **g**_____ up in the morning

6 **w**_____ TV
7 **d**_____ housework
8 **sp**_____ English
9 **h**_____ two children
10 **dr**_____ tea

c Complete the words.

My wife's a **t**_eacher_ in a school in the city.
1 I don't have a job. I'm **u**_____.
2 He's a **w**_____. He works in a restaurant.
3 My grandfather doesn't work now. He's **r**_____.
4 My sister's a **n**_____. She works in a big hospital.
5 He's a **j**_____. He writes for the *New York Times*.

d Write the times.

(a) quarter past ten   1 _____   2 _____

3 _____   4 _____   5 _____

PRONUNCIATION

a Write the words for the sound pictures.

	bike	3	
1		4	
2		5	

b **P p.134–5 Sound Bank** Look at more words with the sounds in **a**, and these sounds:

Practise saying the example words.

c Under<u>line</u> the stressed syllable.

<u>break</u>|fast   2 po|lice|man   4 u|sual|ly

1 po|ta|toes   3 al|ways   5 ce|re|al

CAN YOU understand this text?

a Read the text and complete it with words from the list.

coffee   diet   don't   every   good   hamburgers   meat
potatoes   small   stop   vegetables

EAT THE JAPANESE WAY

Doctors say that the traditional *diet* in Japan and other Asian countries is very healthy.

WHY IS IT GOOD FOR YOU?

In Japan, people don't eat a lot of red ¹_____, butter, or cheese. They eat a lot of rice and fish and fresh fruit and ²_____. This diet is very ³_____ for your heart and people in Japan live longer than in other countries.

HOW TO EAT LIKE THE JAPANESE

◆ Eat rice with your meals and don't eat a lot of ⁴_____, especially chips.

◆ Eat a lot of fish. ⁵_____ eat a lot of meat, for example steak and ⁶_____.

◆ Eat fresh fruit and vegetables ⁷_____ day.

◆ Drink green tea, not ⁸_____.

◆ Eat on ⁹_____ plates. Eat slowly. ¹⁰_____ eating when you are full.

b Do <u>you</u> eat 'the Japanese way'?

CAN YOU understand these people?

◀)6.20 Watch or listen and answer the questions.

1 John   2 Hanna   3 Lisa   4 Susan   5 Kieran

1 For breakfast John usually has ____.
   a tea and cereal
   b tea and toast
   c coffee and toast

2 Hanna lives in ____.
   a a flat in London
   b a house near London
   c a house near Manchester

3 Lisa's son is ____.
   a 1
   b 6
   c 16

4 Susan ____.
   a doesn't work
   b is a taxi driver
   c works in an office

5 Kieran gets up at ____ at weekends.
   a 8 a.m.
   b 9 a.m.
   c 10 a.m.

CAN YOU say this in English?

Tick (✓) the boxes.

Can you...?	Yes, I can.
1 say what you do (your job or activity)	▢
2 ask what other people do	▢
3 say what you have for breakfast	▢
4 say what people eat in your country	▢
5 ask and say what time it is	▢
6 say what you do on a typical day	▢
7 ask about other people's days	▢

What do you do at the weekend?

I usually visit my family.

G word order in questions: *be* and present simple | V common verb phrases 2: free time | P /w/, /h/, /eə/, and /aʊ/

1 READING & LISTENING

a Read the article. Then with a partner, complete it with the percentages in the list.

10% 46% 48% 66% 75%

🔍 % = per cent

Three out of four British people do the same thing every weekend!

After a hard week at work, the weekend is a time to do something fun and exciting. But a new study says that ¹_____ of British people do the same activities every Saturday and Sunday. What do they do? ²_____ watch TV, ³_____ go shopping, and ⁴_____ do housework. And ⁵_____ spend the weekend at home – they never leave the house!

Adapted from the British Press

b 🔊 7.1 Read and listen to the article. Check your answers.

Polly is a hairdresser. She lives in Bristol with her husband, Andrew.

c 🔊 7.2 Listen to Polly talk about her weekend. Are her weekends usually the same?

> **Glossary**
> **Match of the Day** a British Saturday night TV programme about football

d Listen again. When does Polly do these things? Write **Fr** (Friday), **Sa** (Saturday), or **Su** (Sunday).

1 ⬜ She does housework.
2 ⬜ She gets up at 7.30.
3 ⬜ She gets up at about 9.00.
4 *Fr* She goes to the pub with her husband.
5 ⬜ She goes to the supermarket.
6 ⬜ She has lunch with her parents.
7 ⬜ She meets friends.
8 ⬜ She watches TV.
9 ⬜ She works until 4.00 p.m.

e Do you do the same thing every weekend, or are your weekends different?

2 VOCABULARY common verb phrases 2: free time

a Look at some sentences from the interview. Can you remember the missing verbs?

1 My husband Andrew and I always _____ out for a drink or for dinner.
2 We sometimes _____ friends there, too.
3 In the evening we usually _____ at home and watch TV.

b 🔊 7.3 Listen and check.

c V p.126 Vocabulary Bank Common verb phrases 2 Do Part 1.

3 GRAMMAR word order in questions: *be* and present simple

a Re-order the words to make questions. Can you remember Polly's answers?

1 's favourite what your of weekend part the

_____

_____ ?

2 tired Sunday on evening you are

_____

_____ ?

3 Saturday do usually what do you on

_____

_____ ?

4 do do thing weekend every same you the

_____

_____ ?

b Ⓖ p.104 Grammar Bank 7A

4 PRONUNCIATION /w/, /h/, /eə/, and /aʊ/

a ◉7.7 Listen and repeat the words and sounds.

	witch	what when why walk watch always
	house	how home husband holidays who
	chair	hairdresser where there their
	owl	how town out mountains

b ◉7.8 Listen and repeat the conversations. Then practise them with a partner.

A What do you do at the weekend?
B I walk, or I watch TV.

A Who's Henry?
B He's my husband.

A Where do they live?
B Their house is over there.

A How do you relax?
B I go to the mountains near my town.

5 SPEAKING

a Look at the questions. What are the missing words? Think about your answers.

Your weekend

		Your partner
1	/ go out on Friday or Saturday night? Where / go?	
2	/ go shopping on Saturday? Where?	
3	/ do housework at the weekend?	
4	/ do sport or exercise? What / do?	
5	/ watch sport on TV? What / watch?	
6	What time / get up on Sunday?	
7	Where / have lunch?	
8	How / relax at the weekend?	
9	/ usually tired on Sunday evening? Why?	
10	What time / go to bed?	
11	What / your favourite part of the weekend?	

b Ask and answer the questions with a partner. Write your partner's answers.

Do you go out on Friday or Saturday night?

Yes, I usually go out with my friends on Saturday night.

Where do you go?

It depends. To the cinema or to a restaurant…

c Find a new partner. Ask and answer some questions about your old partner's weekend.

Does Marco do sport or exercise at the weekend?

Yes, he does. He goes to the gym on Saturday morning.

WORDS AND PHRASES TO LEARN 7A

p.132 Listen and repeat the words and phrases.

Go online to review the lesson

43

G imperatives, object pronouns: *me, him,* etc. **V** kinds of films **P** sentence rhythm

1 GRAMMAR imperatives, object pronouns: *me, him,* etc.

a ◗)7.10 Read and listen to a film director and some actors. Does Scarlett love Sam? Does she love Rupert?

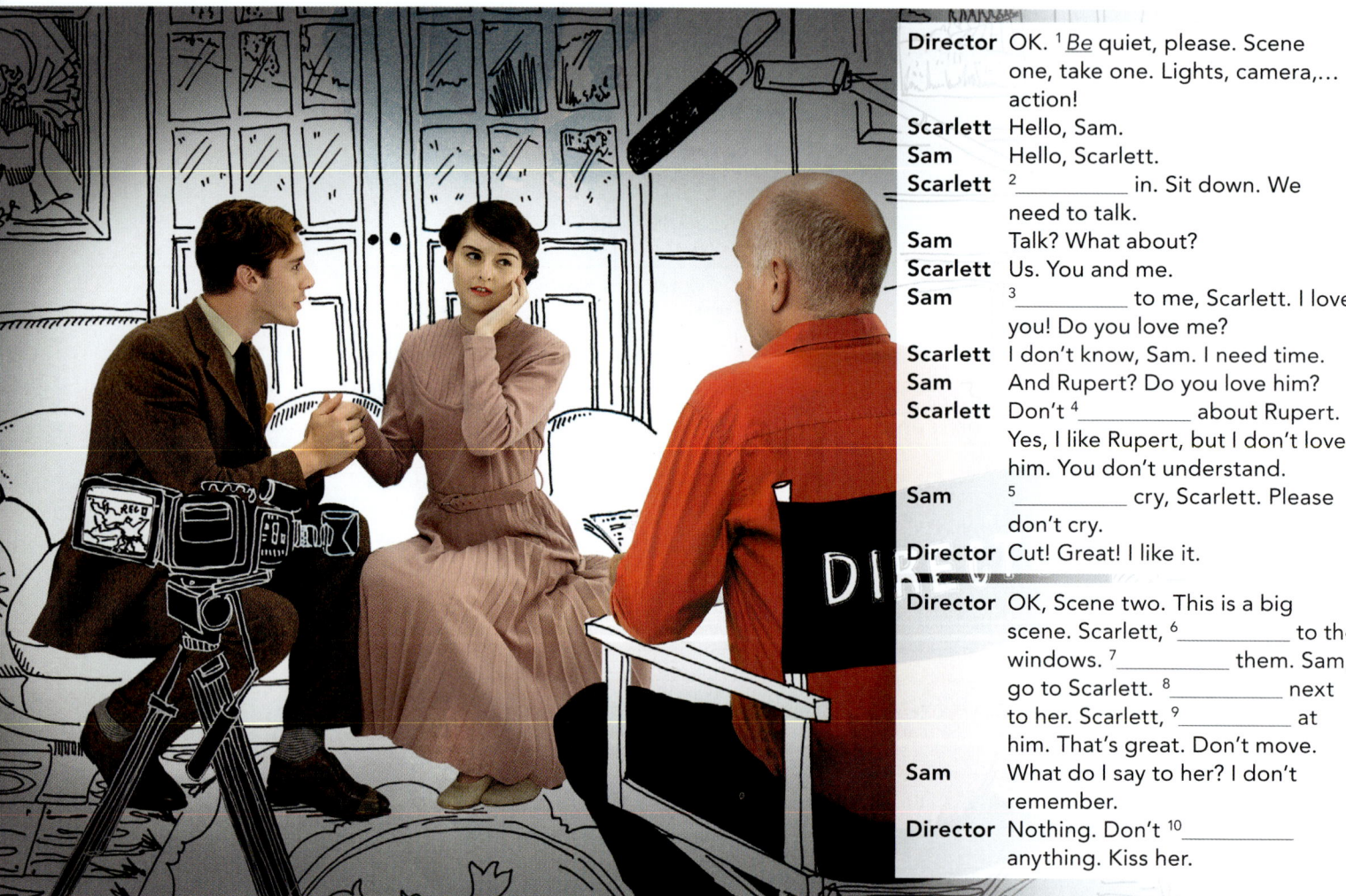

Director	OK. ¹<u>Be</u> quiet, please. Scene one, take one. Lights, camera,... action!
Scarlett	Hello, Sam.
Sam	Hello, Scarlett.
Scarlett	²_____ in. Sit down. We need to talk.
Sam	Talk? What about?
Scarlett	Us. You and me.
Sam	³_____ to me, Scarlett. I love you! Do you love me?
Scarlett	I don't know, Sam. I need time.
Sam	And Rupert? Do you love him?
Scarlett	Don't ⁴_____ about Rupert. Yes, I like Rupert, but I don't love him. You don't understand.
Sam	⁵_____ cry, Scarlett. Please don't cry.
Director	Cut! Great! I like it.
Director	OK, Scene two. This is a big scene. Scarlett, ⁶_____ to the windows. ⁷_____ them. Sam, go to Scarlett. ⁸_____ next to her. Scarlett, ⁹_____ at him. That's great. Don't move.
Sam	What do I say to her? I don't remember.
Director	Nothing. Don't ¹⁰_____ anything. Kiss her.

b Listen again and complete the conversation.

c Cover the conversation. Complete the sentences with the words from the list.

---
him it me me them ~~us~~ you
---

1 'We need to talk.'
  'Talk? What about?'
  '<u>Us</u>.'
2 'Listen to _____, Scarlett.'
3 'I love _____! Do you love _____?'
4 'I like Rupert, but I don't love _____.'
5 'Great! I like _____.'
6 'Go to the windows. Open _____.'

d ◗)7.11 Listen and check.

e **G** p.104 Grammar Bank 7B

f ◗)7.14 Listen and say the object pronoun.

  1 ◗) *I* (*me*

g ◗)7.15 Listen and change the sentence. Use *him, her, it,* or *them.*

  1 ◗) *I love Scarlett.* (*I love her.*

h In groups of three, act out the conversation in **a.**

And Rupert? Do you love him?

Don't talk about Rupert!

2 VOCABULARY kinds of films

a Match the kinds of films 1–7 to film titles A–G.

1 ___ action films
2 ___ animations
3 ___ comedies
4 ___ dramas
5 ___ horror films
6 ___ science fiction films
7 ___ westerns

A Psycho   The Exorcist   Friday the 13th
B The Good, the Bad, and the Ugly   The Magnificent Seven   Django Unchained
C Pinocchio   Toy Story   Frozen
D Skyfall   The Terminator   Tomb Raider
E Meet the Parents   Zoolander   Volver
F Casablanca   The Godfather   Forrest Gump
G Aliens   2001: A Space Odyssey   Avatar

b ◉ 7.16 Listen and check.   **c** ◉ 7.17 Now listen and repeat the kinds of films.

Charlize Theron

3 LISTENING

a Look at the film posters and photos. Do you know the films and the actors?

b ◉ 7.18 Listen to five people answering questions about the Alien films and the actors. Which two speakers like all the films?

c Listen again. Who or what do the **bold** pronouns refer to?

Speaker 1 **It**'s great.
Speaker 2 **She**'s OK, but I prefer Sigourney Weaver.
Speaker 3 I think **they**'re awful.
Speaker 4 I really like **him**. I think **he**'s great.
Speaker 5 Sorry, I don't know **them**.

d Do you like the films and the actors?

4 PRONUNCIATION & SPEAKING sentence rhythm

a ◉ 7.19 Listen and repeat the conversations. <u>Copy</u> the <u>rhy</u>thm.

> A Do you **like** <u>Si</u>gourney <u>Wea</u>ver?
> B **Yes**, I **do**. She's <u>very</u> **good**.

> C Do you **like** <u>ho</u>rror **films**?
> D **No**, I **don't like** them. I **prefer** <u>dra</u>mas.

> E Do you **like** Michael <u>Fass</u>bender?
> F **Yes**, I **like** him a **lot**. I **think** he's **great**.

b Practise the conversations in **a** with a partner.

c Write three kinds of films or film series, three actresses, and three actors in the chart.

Kinds of films or film series	Actresses	Actors

d In pairs, ask and answer questions about the people and kinds of films in the chart.

WORDS AND PHRASES TO LEARN 7B

p.132 Listen and repeat the words and phrases.

Michael Fassbender
PROMETHEUS
ALIEN
In space no one can hear you scream.
Sigourney Weaver

ALIEN
COVENANT

Go online to review the lesson

1 VOCABULARY months

a When are these special days?
Match them to the month.

1 ☐ Christmas Day   A January
2 ☐ New Year's Day   B February
3 ☐ Halloween   C December
4 ☐ Valentine's Day   D November
5 ☐ Thanksgiving   E October

b **V** p.127 **Vocabulary Bank** Months and ordinal numbers Do Part 1.

c Answer the questions in groups.

1 Which month sometimes has 29 days?
2 Which month has only three letters?
3 Which three months begin with the letter J?
4 Which four months end in -er?

2 VOCABULARY & PRONUNCIATION
ordinal numbers; /θ/

a Do the Ordinals quiz with a partner.

b 🔊7.22 Listen and check your answers.

c **V** p.127 **Vocabulary Bank** Months and ordinal numbers Do Part 2.

d 🔊7.25 Listen and repeat the words and sound.

θ thumb	three Thursday third seventh ninth

e 🔊7.26 Listen. Say the ordinal number.

)) one (first

Ordinals quiz

1 What's J.K. Rowling's **first** name?

a Janet
b Joanne
c Juliet

2 What's the **second** meal of the day?

a breakfast
b dinner
c lunch

3 Which is the **third** book in the Lord of the Rings trilogy?

a *The Two Towers*
b *The Return of the King*
c *The Fellowship of the Ring*

4 What's the **fourth** letter on the top row of a keyboard?

a Q   b R   c T

5 Which city has a famous street called **Fifth** Avenue?

a New York
b London
c Sydney

6 Who was the **sixth** president of the USA?

a John Quincy Adams
b Abraham Lincoln
c George Washington

7 Which is the **seventh** Star Wars film?

a *The Return of the Jedi*
b *Rogue One*
c *The Force Awakens*

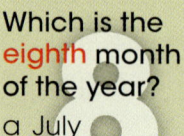

8 Which is the **eighth** month of the year?

a July
b August
c September

9 The **Ninth** Legion was a group of soldiers from…

a Rome
b Greece
c Turkey

3 ▶ SAYING THE DATE

a **◀)) 7.27** Watch or listen to Rob talking to his friend Alan. Complete the conversation.

Rob	What's the date today?
Alan	I think it's the [1]_____ of June.
Rob	Are you sure? Isn't it the [2]_____?
Alan	No, definitely the [3]_____.
Rob	Oh no! It's my dad's [4]_____.

b Watch or listen again and repeat the conversation. Then practise it with a partner.

c **◀)) 7.28** Watch or listen to Rob and answer the questions.

1 Where does Rob go?
2 What does he give his father?
3 When is his father's birthday?

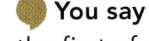
Saying the date

🗣 **You say**	✏ **You write**		
the first of April	1st April	1 April	1/4
the second of June	2nd June	2 June	2/6
the twenty-third of March	23rd March	23 March	23/3
the fourth of May	4th May	4 May	4/5
the twentieth of July	20th July	20 July	20/7

d **◀)) 7.29** Watch or listen and repeat the dates. Practise saying them.

1st January	11th May	22nd September
2nd February	14th June	23rd October
8th March	18th July	30th November
9th April	20th August	31st December

e Ask and answer with a partner.

1 What's the date today?
2 What's the date tomorrow?
3 What other dates are holidays in your town (country)?

f Stand up. Ask other students: *When's your birthday?* Make a class list.

g Tell a partner three birthdays that are important to **you**.

> *My girlfriend's birthday is the second of September.*

4 ▶ TALKING ON THE PHONE

a **◀)) 7.30** Watch or listen. Why does Rob phone Jenny?

b Watch or listen again. Mark the sentences **T** (true) or **F** (false).

1 Rob thinks Jenny arrives in London on 20th March.
2 He thinks she leaves on the 29th.
3 It's Thanksgiving in the USA.
4 Jenny is with her friends.
5 Rob needs to call Jenny on Tuesday 1st December.

5 ▶ USEFUL PHRASES

◀)) 7.31 Watch or listen and repeat the useful phrases.

What's the date today?
Are you sure?
Isn't it the 1st?
It's my dad's birthday.
This is for you.
Happy Birthday!
Is that Jennifer Zielinski?
Yes. Who's that?
We need to talk about your trip to London.
Of course!
Call me on Monday at work.
Talk to you on Tuesday.

Can you come on Monday at 8.30?

No, I can't, but I can come at 10.00.

G can / can't   **V** more verb phrases   **P** can / can't: /ə/, /æ/, and /ɑː/, sentence rhythm

1 READING & VOCABULARY

a Read the text and complete the sentences with a country from the list.

Mexico   Pakistan   South Africa
the UK   the USA

DRIVING ROUND THE WORLD

1 In some states in _____, for example Kansas and Idaho, you can have a driving licence when you're 14.

2 In some cities in _____, you don't need to take a test to get a driving licence, you only need to be 18.

3 In _____, you can drive when you are 17. First you need to pass a theory test and then you have a practical test. 47% of people pass first time.

4 In _____, the driving test is very difficult. Only 3% pass first time.

5 In _____, the driving test is very easy and not many people fail. You can take the theory test and the practical test on the same day.

b 🔊 8.1 Listen and check.

c 🔊 8.2 Listen and repeat the highlighted phrases. What's the situation in your country?

In Colombia you can have a driving licence when you're 16.

2 GRAMMAR can / can't

a Anna wants to learn to drive. Match her tweets to photos 1–3.

A Anna Jones @annaj • Jul 19
Dad's a terrible teacher. I need some practical lessons with a GOOD driving instructor! Friends, can you help?

B Anna Jones @annaj • Jul 18
A pass in the theory – fantastic! 🙂 My first lesson with Dad – total disaster! 😮 Now Dad says I can't practise in his car 🙁.

C Anna Jones @annaj • Apr 23
The theory test is very difficult. I can practise online, but I can't answer the questions. 'Can you park on a yellow line?' I don't know!

b 🔊 8.3 Listen and check.

c 🔊 8.4 Listen to Anna phoning a driving instructor. Complete the conversation with verbs from the list.

book   come (x2)   help   meet   start

Instructor	Hello, can I ¹_____ you?
Anna	Yes, can I ²_____ some driving lessons, please?
Instructor	Yes, of course.
Anna	When can I ³_____?
Instructor	I'm free on Monday. We can ⁴_____ at your house.
Anna	Can you ⁵_____ at 8.30?
Instructor	No, sorry, I can't. I have a lesson at 8.00.
Anna	OK… Can you ⁶_____ at 10.00?
Instructor	Yes, I can. The lessons are one hour, so 10.00 to 11.00, OK?
Anna	Great!
Instructor	What's your name and address?
Anna	It's Anna Jones…

d 🔊 8.5 After three months, Anna takes her driving test. Listen. Does she pass?

e Read the tweets and the conversation again. Complete the chart.

can / can't	
+	I _can_ practise online.
−	I _____ answer the questions.
?	_____ you come at 8.30?
✓	Yes, I _____ .
✗	No, I _____ .

f Ⓖ p.106 Grammar Bank 8A

3 PRONUNCIATION & LISTENING can / can't: /ə/, /æ/, and /ɑː/, sentence rhythm

a 🔊 8.7 Listen and repeat the sounds and sentences. Copy the rhythm.

💻 computer	Where c**a**n I **park**? You c**a**n **park here**.
🐱 cat	Can I **park here**? **Yes**, you c**a**n.
🚗 car	**No**, you c**a**n't. You **can't park here**.

b 🔊 8.8 Listen to the difference between _can_ and _can't_.

1 a We can park here.   b We can't park here.
2 a I can help you.   b I can't help you.
3 a You can sit here.   b You can't sit here.
4 a Max can go with me.   b Max can't go with me.

c 🔊 8.9 Listen. Circle a or b.

d Practise the conversation in **2c** with a partner.

e 🔊 8.10 Listen to four conversations. Where are the people?

1 on a _____   3 in a _____
2 in a _____   4 in the _____

4 VOCABULARY more verb phrases

a What do these signs mean? Complete the sentences with _can / can't_ and a verb from the list.

| change   drive   have   park   pay   play |
| ~~swim~~   take   use (x2) |

1 You _can't_ _swim_ here.
2 You _____ _____ by credit card here.
3 You _____ _____ your mobile phone here.
4 You _____ _____ here.
5 You _____ _____ a coffee here.
6 You _____ _____ the internet here.
7 You _____ _____ photos here.
8 You _____ _____ football here.
9 You _____ _____ money here.
10 You _____ _____ fast here.

b 🔊 8.11 Listen and check.

c Cover the sentences and look at the signs. Say what they mean.

5 SPEAKING & WRITING

a Ⓒ **Communication** I'm a tourist. Where can I...?
A p.80 B p.84 Ask questions about places in a town.

b Write four sentences to give tourists some useful information about what you can (or can't) do in <u>your</u> town.

You can buy fantastic fruit in the market.

WORDS AND PHRASES TO LEARN 8A

p.132 Listen and repeat the words and phrases.

> Do you like camping?

> No, I hate it. I like sleeping in a bed!

1 VOCABULARY activities

a What are the activities in the photos? Complete the missing letters.

1 r____ ____ ____ing
2 s____ ____ ____ming
3 c____ ____ ____ing

b **V** p.128 **Vocabulary Bank** Activities

2 GRAMMAR *like / love / hate + verb + -ing*

a Read the profiles of six people from a dating website. In pairs, match the women and men. Say why.

1 Isabella and _____
2 Angie and _____
3 Adriana and _____

> *Isabella and… Because he loves…and she likes…*

b Number the verbs 1–4, from very positive (1) to very negative (4).

☐ don't like ☐ hate ☐ like ☐ love

c **G** p.106 **Grammar Bank 8B**

Do you like what I like?

Isabella
- ❤ I love playing the piano.
- ✓ I like doing sport.
- ✗ I don't like travelling.

William
- ❤ I love running and cycling.
- ✓ I like classical music.
- ✗ ✗ I hate flying.

Angie
- ❤ I love buying clothes.
- ✓ I like the cinema.
- ✗ I don't like reading.

Daniel
- ❤ I love cooking.
- ✓ I like camping.
- ✗ I don't like watching TV.

Adriana
- ❤ I love walking in the mountains.
- ✓ I like good food.
- ✗ ✗ I hate shopping.

Luke
- ❤ I love shopping.
- ✓ I like watching films.
- ✗ I don't like sport.

3 PRONUNCIATION & SPEAKING
/ʊ/, /uː/, and /ŋ/, sentence rhythm

a 🔊 8.15 Listen and repeat the words and sounds.

🐂 bull	book cook look good
👢 boot	too food soon school
🎵 singer	do**ing** go**ing** swimm**ing** thi**ng**

b 🔊 8.16 Listen and repeat the conversation. Practise it in pairs. Copy the sounds and <u>rhythm</u>.

A I **love** <u>cooking</u>. What <u>about</u> you?
B I **like** <u>cooking</u>, too.
A Do you **like** <u>reading books</u>?
B Yes, I **like** <u>reading good books</u>.
A Do you **like** <u>cycling</u>?
B Yes, I **do**. I **love** <u>cycling</u>!
A Are you **single**?
B No, <u>sorry</u>.

c In pairs, talk about the activities in **Vocabulary Bank** Activities **p.128** Use *love, like, don't like,* or *hate.*

I love buying clothes. What about you?

Me too! I hate camping. What about you?

4 READING & WRITING

a Read the tweets and complete the missing activities.

What do you like doing alone?
What do you like doing with friends?

Chris I like c<u>ooking</u> alone. I don't like having other people in the kitchen. But I like ¹e_____ with friends, especially when I'm out. I don't like being alone in a restaurant. #aloneorwithfriends?

Sarah I don't like ²tr_____ alone – I prefer going on holiday with friends. But they need to be the right friends! #aloneorwithfriends?

Mike I like ³sh_____ with friends. When I go alone, I usually buy things that look horrible on me. I need a second opinion! #aloneorwithfriends?

Greta I love ⁴d_____ alone at home to really old music from the 70s, like Abba. But I never dance with other people at parties because I know I'm a terrible dancer. #aloneorwithfriends?

Veronica I like ⁵w_____ films with friends. When the film finishes, we can talk about it, and I like having someone with me so we can be happy or frightened together! #aloneorwithfriends?

Becca I like ⁶r_____ alone. It helps me to concentrate and it's very peaceful! But I prefer ⁷g_____ for walks with other people because I like walking and talking. #aloneorwithfriends?

Andy I like ⁸dr_____ alone. I love ⁹l_____ to my favourite music in the car and ¹⁰s_____ very loudly – but with the windows closed, of course! #aloneorwithfriends?

b 🔊 8.17 Listen and check. Tick (✓) two people you agree with.

c Compare with a partner. Did you choose the same people?

d Write your answer to the two questions and give it to your teacher. Play *Guess who?*

5 ▶ VIDEO LISTENING Singing in a choir

a Watch the video once. Do you like the song?

b Watch it again and complete the sentences with one word.
1 The choir's name is The _____ Gargoyles.
2 The choir has _____ members.
3 They are all _____ at Oxford University.
4 They all study music except _____.
5 They practise on _____ and _____.
6 They practise for _____ hours.
7 They give concerts once a _____.
8 They give concerts in _____, theatres, and churches.
9 Steph loves singing _____ and opera.
10 Freddie thinks everyone can sing because everyone can _____.
11 Steph likes singing because she feels _____ when she sings.
12 Tegan prefers singing in a _____.

WORDS AND PHRASES TO LEARN 8B

p.132 Listen and repeat the words and phrases.

🔵 **Go online** to watch the video and review the lesson

GRAMMAR

Circle a or b.

_____'s your name?
a Who   b **What**

1 A _____ do any sport or exercise?
   B No, I hate sport.
   a Do you   b Are you

2 What music _____?
   a you like   b do you like

3 Where's _____?
   a your mother from   b from your mother

4 _____ meat?
   a Your sister eats   b Does your sister eat

5 The meeting's at 6.00. _____ late.
   a Don't be   b Not be

6 We're lost. Please help _____.
   a us   b our

7 My brother has a new girlfriend, but I don't like _____ very much.
   a him   b her

8 They're beautiful shoes. I love _____.
   a it   b them

9 _____ park here?
   a Can I   b Do I can

10 Sorry, you _____ photos here.
   a can't to take   b can't take

11 A Can they come to dinner tomorrow?
   B No, they _____.
   a can't   b don't

12 _____ Lisa sit here?
   a Can   b Cans

13 Do you like _____?
   a read   b reading

14 I don't like _____ up early.
   a geting   b getting

15 I hate _____ at the weekend.
   a studying   b studing

VOCABULARY

a Complete the verbs.

For my mum's birthday, I always **m**ake a big chocolate cake.

1 I always **pl**_____ computer games after school.
2 Can I **p**_____ by credit card?
3 In summer, we **w**_____ in the mountains, but in the winter we **sk**_____.
4 I sometimes **m**_____ my friends after work and we **g**_____ to the cinema.
5 Mary doesn't usually **g**_____ to the beach because she can't **sw**_____.
6 I **d**_____ a lot of sport – I **pl**_____ tennis every week.

b Write the next word.

first, second, *third*
1 fifth, sixth, _____
2 tenth, eleventh, _____
3 eighteenth, nineteenth, _____
4 twenty-ninth, thirtieth, _____

5 January, February, _____
6 March, April, _____
7 May, June, _____
8 September, October, _____

c Write the activities.

cycling   1 _____   2 _____   3 _____

4 _____   5 _____   6 _____   7 _____

PRONUNCIATION

a Write the words for the sound pictures.

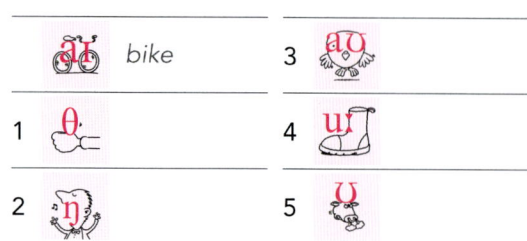

🚲 *bike*	3 🦉
1 👍	4 👢
2 🐑	5 🐑

b 🅿 p.134–5 Sound Bank Look at more words with the sounds in in **a**, and these sounds:

Practise saying the example words.

c Underline the stressed syllable.

re|<u>lax</u>   1 thir|ti|eth   2 Jan|u|ary   3 Ju|ly   4 se|ven|teen   5 sing|le

CAN YOU understand this text?

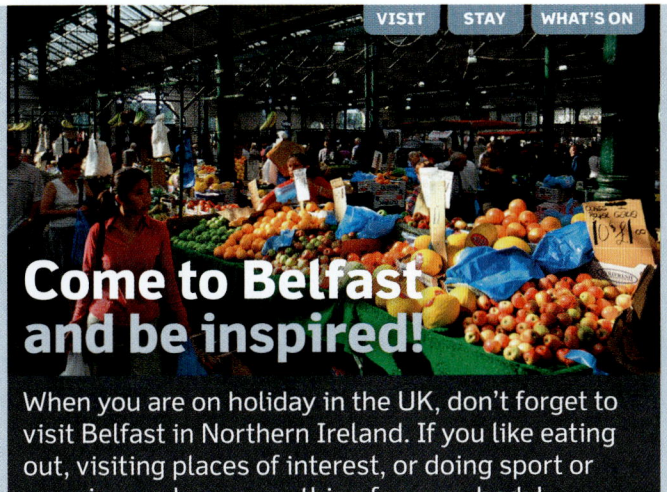

VISIT STAY WHAT'S ON

Come to Belfast and be inspired!

When you are on holiday in the UK, don't forget to visit Belfast in Northern Ireland. If you like eating out, visiting places of interest, or doing sport or exercise, we have something for everybody!

1 _____

This is one of Belfast's oldest attractions. Here you can try all kinds of different local food, and if you like cooking, you can buy wonderful products to take home. You can also listen to live music. The market is open on Friday, Saturday, and Sunday.

2 _____

The museum is situated next to the place where this great ship was made, just ten minutes from the city centre. You can learn all about the history of the *Titanic*, from its construction to its tragic end. You can also have lunch (but not dinner) at one of the museum's luxury restaurants, which are copies of the restaurants on the *Titanic*.

3 _____

Northern Ireland is famous for its golfers, like Rory McIlroy and Darren Clarke. Belfast has 14 golf courses and the famous courses of Royal County Down and Royal Portrush are only an hour from Belfast by car.

a Read the website and match the headings.

World-class golf   St George's Market
The *Titanic* museum

b Read again and tick (✓) if you can find the information.

1 ☐ You can buy very cheap food in the market.
2 ☐ Musicians play in the market.
3 ☐ You can only go to the market at weekends.
4 ☐ The *Titanic* museum is a very new museum.
5 ☐ The restaurants in the museum don't open in the evening.
6 ☐ Rory McIlroy teaches golf at one of the golf courses.
7 ☐ You can drive to two world-famous golf courses.

▶ CAN YOU understand these people?

◀) 8.19 Watch or listen and answer the questions.

| 1 Spencer | 2 Sahil | 3 Susan | 4 Nell | 5 Richard |

1 Spencer usually _____ in the evening.
   a does sport
   b does housework
   c makes dinner
2 Sahil likes watching _____ in the cinema
   a comedy films
   b action films
   c animations
3 Susan's birthday is on _____.
   a 5th April
   b 15th April
   c 5th May
4 Nell usually drives _____.
   a to the park
   b her husband's car
   c to her office
5 One thing Richard likes doing at the weekend is _____.
   a running
   b making meals
   c buying clothes

CAN YOU say this in English?

Tick (✓) the boxes.

Can you...?	Yes, I can.
1 talk about what you do in your free time	☐
2 give instructions and orders, e.g. 'Sit down.'	☐
3 talk about films and actors that you like	☐
4 say the date	☐
5 say what people can / can't do in your town	☐
6 talk about activities you like / love / hate doing	☐

🔄 **Go online** to watch the video, review Files 7 & 8, and check your progress

G present continuous   **V** common verb phrases 2: travelling   **P** sentence rhythm

> **What are you doing?**
> **I'm playing a video game.**

1 GRAMMAR present continuous

a 🔊 **9.1** Carol is in Switzerland on business. Her husband and family are at home in the UK. Listen to and read the conversation. <u>Underline</u> three things Tony says which are not true.

Carol	Hello? Tony?
Tony	Oh, hi, darling. How's Zurich?
Carol	Fine, fine. I'm staying in a nice hotel – but it's raining. Can you hear it?
Tony	Yes, yes, I can.
Carol	How are the children?
Tony	Oh, they're fine.
Carol	Where are they? What are they doing?
Tony	Lily's in the living room. She's doing her homework.
Carol	And Matt and Josh?
Tony	They're in their bedroom. They're reading.
Carol	I think I can hear them. Are you sure they're reading?
Tony	Yes, yes. That noise is the TV. Your mother's watching a film.
Carol	What about you? Are you OK?
Tony	I'm fine. I'm making dinner – fish and vegetables.
Carol	Oh great! Very healthy. OK darling, I need to go now. See you on Tuesday.
Tony	Have a good day tomorrow. Bye.

b Look at the highlighted verbs in the conversation. Then read the rule below and circle a or b.

> We use the present continuous (*am* / *is* / *are* + verb + *-ing*) to talk about **a** every day, **b** now.

c **G** p.108 **Grammar Bank 9A**

d 🔊 **9.3** Listen. What's Tony doing this evening?

> 1 *He's reading a story.*

e Think about <u>your</u> home. Who do you think is there? Where are they? What are they doing?

> *I think my brother's in his bedroom. He's sleeping.*

bedroom

living room

kitchen

2 PRONUNCIATION sentence rhythm

a ◖9.4 Listen and repeat the conversation.

> A **What** are you **doing**?
> B I'm **making dinner**.
> A Are the **children doing** their **homework**?
> B **No**, they **aren't**. They're **watching** TV.
> A **What's** your **mother doing**?
> B She's **helping** me.

b Practise the conversation in **1a** with a partner.

c Look at pictures 1–6. Ask and answer the questions with a partner.

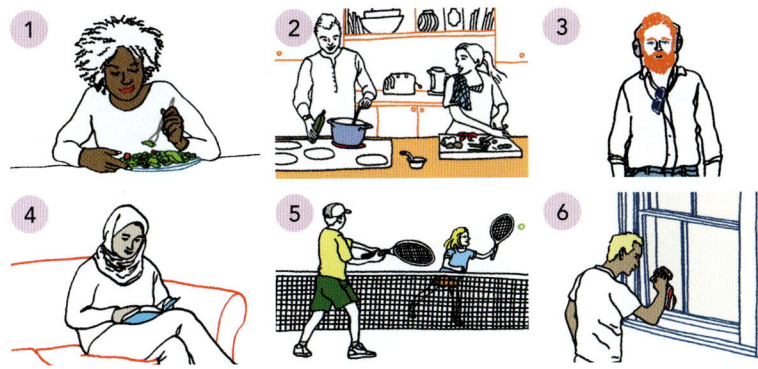

Picture 1. What's she doing? *She's…*

Picture 2. What are they doing? *They're…*

3 VOCABULARY & LISTENING common verb phrases 2: travelling

a Look at the picture of Carol in **1a**. Complete the missing verbs.

1 Carol is **st**_____ in a hotel.
2 She's **ph**_____ her husband.

b Ⓥ p.126 **Vocabulary Bank** Common verb phrases 2 Do Part 2.

c ◖9.6 Listen to four conversations. What are the people doing?

1 The man and the woman are _____.
2 The woman is _____.
3 The man _____.
4 The man and the woman _____.

d Listen again and ⃝circle the correct answer.

1 Johnny's present is a *football / football shirt* and Jessica's is a *bag / T-shirt*.
2 Their hotel *has / doesn't have* a swimming pool.
3 The man is interested in a *small / big* manual car for *three / five* days.
4 The first bus is a number *23 / 25*. They are waiting for a number *13 / 30*.

4 READING

a Mike and Lina are going to the cinema together. Read Mike's messages to Lina. Then match her answers to each message 1–5.

1 ☐ Hi. I'm just leaving the house now.

2 ☐ No, I'm not. I'm cycling. See you in 20 minutes?

3 ☐ Where are you? I'm at the cinema, but I can't see you. I'm waiting outside.

4 ☐ It's really cold outside. I'm going in.

5 ☐ I'm standing near the box office. I'm wearing a black jacket. Can you see me?

A I'm arriving at the cinema now. Where are you?

B Me too. I'm walking to the bus stop. Are you getting the bus, too?

C Sorry, we're in a lot of traffic. There in five minutes.

D OK. See you then.

E Yes, I can! Can you see me? I'm walking towards you now!

b ◖9.7 Listen and check.

c Read the messages again. Find a word or phrase which means:

1 the place where you wait for a bus: _____
2 the opposite of *inside*: _____
3 a lot of cars, buses, etc.: a lot of _____
4 the place where you buy cinema tickets: _____
5 to walk in the direction of somebody: to walk _____ somebody

d ◖9.8 Listen and check.

5 SPEAKING

Ⓒ **Communication** The same or different? **A p.80 B p.84** Say what the people are doing in the pictures.

WORDS AND PHRASES TO LEARN 9A

p.132 Listen and repeat the words and phrases.

Ⓠ **Go online** to review the lesson

What are you doing today?

I usually go to the office, but today I'm working at home.

1 READING

a Look at the two photos of David Clarke. Where do you think he usually works? Where is he working today?

b 🔊 9.10 Read and listen to a text about the British TV show *Undercover Boss*. Why is David working undercover?

c 🔊 9.11 Read and listen to the Episode 1 summary. Mark the sentences **T** (true) or **F** (false).

1 The workers don't know that 'Andy' is their boss.
2 On Monday, David is cooking in the kitchen.
3 The people in the kitchen work long hours.
4 He likes the food in the hotel.
5 On Tuesday, the workers are repairing things in all the rooms.
6 On Wednesday, David is making breakfast.
7 The workers only have 30 minutes to clean rooms.
8 David thinks that cleaning rooms is easy.

d What do you think David does on Friday? Turn to **p.85 Communication** *Undercover Boss* and check.

e Do you think *Undercover Boss* is a good idea for a TV programme?

Undercover Boss

Undercover Boss is a TV show where different bosses work undercover. They want to know more about their workers and about problems in their companies. In **Episode 1**, David Clarke, the manager of a big hotel chain, is working 'undercover' for a week in one of his hotels.

Episode 1 summary

One of the ovens is broken.

Monday David says that he's a new worker and that his name is 'Andy'. The other workers don't know who he really is. He usually wears a suit, but today he's wearing jeans and a T-shirt. He's working in the kitchen – he's washing the dishes. The people in the kitchen usually work 80 hours a week! One of the ovens is broken, but David thinks that the food is good.

Tuesday Today, he's working in the bedrooms. Next week, there is a hotel inspection. The workers are repairing things that are broken, but only in the rooms for the hotel inspector. They aren't repairing things in the other rooms. David isn't happy about this, but he can't say anything.

Wednesday Today, David is working in the restaurant. He's serving breakfast. He's wearing a white jacket and a hat. The waiters and waitresses always work very hard.

Thursday David is cleaning rooms. The workers only have a quarter of an hour to clean a room. David is working very hard. He's very tired.

2 GRAMMAR present continuous or present simple?

a Look at two sentences about David Clarke. Complete the sentences with the present simple or continuous of *work* and *wear*.

He usually ¹*works* in an office, but today he ²_____ in a hotel. He usually ³_____ a suit, but today he ⁴_____ jeans and a T-shirt.

b 🔊 9.12 Listen and check.

c Complete the rules with *every day* and *today / now*.

Use the present simple to talk about _____.
Use the present continuous to talk about _____.

d Ⓖ p.108 **Grammar Bank 9B**

3 VOCABULARY & PRONUNCIATION clothes; /ɜː/, other vowel sounds

a Look at some clothes words from the text in **1**. Match them to the photos.

| ▢ a hat | ▢ a jacket | ▢ jeans | ▢ a suit | ▢ a T-shirt |

b Ⓥ p.129 **Vocabulary Bank** Clothes

c 🔊 9.15 Listen and repeat the words and sound.

₃ː bird	sh**ir**t sk**ir**t T-sh**ir**t s**er**ve w**or**k

d Put the clothes words in the correct column.

c**a**p c**oa**t dr**e**ss h**a**t j**a**cket j**ea**ns sh**oe**s s**ui**t sw**ea**ter tr**ou**sers

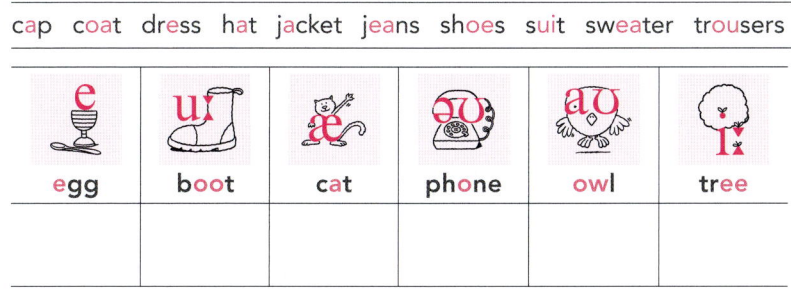

egg	boot	cat	phone	owl	tree

e 🔊 9.16 Listen and check.

f Practise saying the sentences.

I'm wearing…
a sh**ir**t and a sk**ir**t   an **o**ld c**oa**t   clean j**ea**ns
a r**e**d sw**ea**ter   a bl**a**ck j**a**cket br**ow**n tr**ou**sers
a n**ew** s**ui**t   blue sh**oe**s

4 LISTENING & SPEAKING

In secondary schools in the UK, students aged 16–17 do two weeks' work experience. Sandra is working as a shop assistant at a clothes shop called FatFace in London.

a Look at the photos and read about Sandra. Do secondary school students do work experience in your country?

b 🔊 9.17 Listen to an interview with Sandra. Is she positive or negative about her work experience?

c Listen again and answer the questions.

1 What kinds of clothes does FatFace have?
2 What does Sandra do in the shop?
3 What does Sandra like about the job?
4 What doesn't she like?
5 What can Sandra do when she finishes her work experience?
6 Where are the clothes she is wearing today from?

d Talk to a partner.

1 What are you wearing today?
2 What colours do you like wearing?
3 What clothes do you usually wear…?
  – in the summer
  – in the winter
  – to work / school
  – for a party

WORDS AND PHRASES TO LEARN 9B

p.132 Listen and repeat the words and phrases.

1 ▶ INVITING AND OFFERING

a 🔊 9.19 Watch or listen. Number the photos 1–3.

b Watch or listen again and complete the conversations.

1 Rob   Hey, Alan. **Would you like** to come to the ¹_____ with me on ²_____? It's Norwich against Chelsea, and I have two tickets.
   Alan   Wow! What time's the match?
   Rob   It's at ³_____.
   Alan   Yeah, I'd love to. Thanks.
   Rob   **Would you like** to meet for ⁴_____ first?
   Alan   Sorry, I can't. It's my mum's ⁵_____, and I need to have lunch with her. But I can meet you there.
   Rob   Great. Let's meet at ⁶_____ at the entrance to the Tube station.
   Alan   Fine. See you there.

2 Alan   They are playing really badly. I hope the second half is better.
   Rob   Me too. I ⁷_____ they can win. **Would you like** a ⁸_____?
   Alan   No, thanks. I'm not very ⁹_____.
   Rob   How about a ¹⁰_____?
   Alan   Yeah, great.

   Rob   A burger and a ¹¹_____, please.
   Alan   And **I'd like** a ¹²_____.
   Barman ¹³_____ and sugar?
   Alan   Yes, please.

Glossary
the entrance the door where you go into a place
the Tube the underground train in London

---

c Look at the <mark>highlighted</mark> phrases in the conversations. What do you think *Would you like?* and *I'd like* mean?

🔍 *Would you like...?*

Would you *like* + noun
Would you like a burger?
Yes, please.   No, thanks.
I'd like (= I would like) + noun
I'd like a burger, please.
I'd like a coffee, please.

Would you like to + verb
Would you like to come to the match?
Yes, I'd love to.   Sorry, I can't.
❗ **Compare**
Do you like dancing? = in general
Would you like to dance? = invitation

2 PRONUNCIATION sentence rhythm

a ◀9.20 Watch or listen and repeat.

a pizza
  ↘ *like a pizza*
      ↘ *Would you **like** a pizza?*

see a film
  ↘ *to **see** a film*
      ↘ *Would you **like** to **see** a film?*

b Work in pairs. Use the photos. Ask a partner.

(*Would you like a...?*

(*Would you like to go to a...?*

c In pairs, practise the conversations in **1b**. Change roles.

3 ▶ MEETING AN OLD FRIEND

a ◀9.21 Jenny meets her ex-boyfriend Steve, a journalist, in the street. Watch or listen. What three things does Steve invite Jenny to do?

b Watch or listen again. Circle the right answer.

1 Jenny is looking *well / tired*.
2 It's *raining / starting to rain* in the street.
3 Jenny's meeting is in *half an hour / an hour*.
4 Jenny *can / can't* go to the exhibition.
5 Jenny thinks it *is / isn't* a good idea to meet Steve one evening.

4 ▶ USEFUL PHRASES

◀9.22 Watch or listen and repeat the useful phrases.

Would you like to come to the match with me?
Yeah, I'd love to.
Let's meet at half past three.
See you there.
Would you like a burger?
How about a coffee?
I'd like to ask you something.
I don't think it's a good idea.

5 SPEAKING & WRITING

a ◀9.23 Listen and repeat the conversations. Then practise them with a partner.

1 A Would you like to come to a party at my house?
  B Yes, I'd love to. Thanks! When is it?
  A It's on Friday at 8.00.
  B Great! See you there.

2 A Would you like to come to a party on Saturday?
  B Sorry, I can't. I'm busy on Saturday night.

b Imagine it's <u>your</u> party. Choose a day and time. Invite your partner. Can he or she come?

c Invite the other students in your class. How many people can come?

d ⓦp.87 **Writing** An email Write an email to invite someone to do something.

Is there a restaurant?

No, there isn't, but there are some pubs in the village.

1 READING & VOCABULARY hotels

a 🔊 10.1 Read and listen to the tourist information about Scotland and Loch Ness. Would you like to go to Scotland? What would you like to see and do there?

VISIT SCOTLAND

Scotland is one of the world's top tourist destinations, with 10,000 km of coast, 790 islands, more than 30,000 'lochs' (the word in Scotland for lakes), famous castles, and beautiful cities. There's something for visitors of all ages.

WHY LOCH NESS?

Loch Ness is 10 km south west of the city of Inverness – perfect for day trips.

You can take a boat trip on the loch and visit the Loch Ness Centre to find out all about 'Nessie', the monster.

One of the most beautiful castles in the world, Urquhart Castle, is on the banks of the loch.

There are wonderful places for walking and cycling very near.

ACCOMMODATION

Stay at the **Craigdarroch Inn**. It's the perfect place for a great view of the loch.

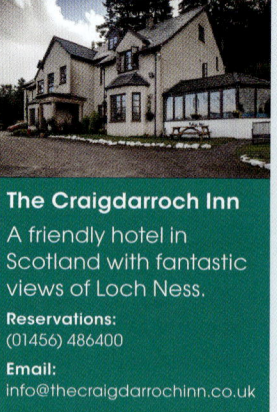

The Craigdarroch Inn

A friendly hotel in Scotland with fantastic views of Loch Ness.

Reservations:
(01456) 486400

Email:
info@thecraigdarrochinn.co.uk

b Look at the hotel bedroom. Match the words to 1–5.

☐ a bed   ☐ a chair   ☐ a mirror   ☐ a picture   ☐ a window

c 🟢 p.130 **Vocabulary Bank** Hotels

2 GRAMMAR *there's a… / there are some…*

a 🔊 10.4 Louisa and Eric are tourists on holiday in Scotland. They arrive at the Craigdarroch Inn. Listen and tick (✓) the things the hotel has and cross (✗) the things it doesn't have.

✗ a lift	☐ a good view	☐ TV	☐ wi-fi
☐ a restaurant	☐ a bar	☐ shops near	

b Listen again and read the conversation on p.61. Look at the highlighted phrases. Circle a or b in the three sentences below. How do you make questions and negatives with *There is / There are*?

1 Use *there's a / an* +
   a singular nouns   b plural nouns.
2 Use *there are some* +
   a singular nouns   b plural nouns.
3 Use *any* (not *some*) in:
   a positive sentences
   b negative sentences and questions.

c 🔊 10.5 Listen. What do Louisa and Eric see? What do they do? Do you think that there's a monster in the lake?

d 🟢 p.110 **Grammar Bank 10A**

e Practise the conversation in **2b** in groups of three.

f In pairs, write true ⊞ or ⊟ sentences.

Your classroom

TV   pictures   windows   whiteboard   DVD player   computer   chairs   dictionaries

Your school

library   café   car park   garden

There's a TV.   There are some pictures.

There aren't any windows.

Eric Hello. Do you have a room for tonight?

Receptionist Let's see. Yes, there's a room on the second floor.

Louisa Great. Can we see it?

R Of course. Come with me.

E Is there a lift?

R I'm sorry, no, there isn't. But I can help you with your cases.

R This is the room.

L It's beautiful. I love it.

E Yes, and there's a great view of Loch Ness.

R The remote control for the TV is on the table.

E Is there wi-fi?

R Yes, there is. There's wi-fi in every room in the hotel. This is the bathroom. There's a bath and a shower.

E Is there a restaurant? We're very hungry.

R No, there isn't a restaurant, sir. But you can have a sandwich in the bar, or there are some pubs in the village.

L Are there any shops near here?

R No, madam, there aren't any shops near the hotel.

E OK, thanks. I have one more question.

R Yes, sir?

E Is there really a monster in Loch Ness?

R Well, some people say there is and some people say there isn't. Enjoy your stay. Breakfast is at 8.00.

3 PRONUNCIATION /ɪə/ and /eə/

a ◗) 10.7 Listen and repeat the words and sounds.

/ɪə/	ear	near here
/eə/	chair	wear there

🔍 **Same spelling, different sound**
The same letters can have different pronunciations, e.g. *ere* and *ear* can be /ɪə/ e.g. *here*, *near*, or /eə/ e.g. *there*, *wear*.

b ◗) 10.8 Listen and write the words in the correct row.

airport beer dear idea really repair their
we're where year

c ◗) 10.9 Listen and check. Practise saying the words.

d Practise saying the sentences.

Here's your beer, dear.   There's a chair over there.
That's a really good idea.   Where's the airport?

4 VOCABULARY & SPEAKING
in, on, under

a Write *in*, *on*, or *under* for pictures 1–3.

1 _____   2 _____   3 _____

b In pairs, ask and answer questions about the remote control.

Picture 1: Where's the remote control? (*It's on the table.*

c ⓒ **Communication** Is there a TV? Where is it?
A p.80 B p.84 Ask and answer about things in hotel rooms.

WORDS AND PHRASES TO LEARN 10A

p.132 Listen and repeat the words and phrases.

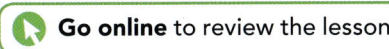
Go online to review the lesson

61

Where were you?

I was at home.

G past simple: *be* **V** *in, on, at* **P** *was* and *were*, sentence rhythm

1 GRAMMAR past simple: *be*

a Last night there was a robbery in a bank. Jason Brown is a suspect. Look at the photo. Which person is Jason, which person is a detective?

b 🔊10.11 Listen to the interview. Complete the gaps.

> **D** Where were you at ¹_____ o'clock last night?
> **J** I was at ²_____.
> **D** You weren't at ³_____. Your ⁴_____ says you were out. She was at home alone.
> **J** Oh yes, I remember now. I was in a ⁵_____.
> **D** Were you ⁶_____?
> **J** No, I wasn't. I was with a ⁷_____. Kevin Smith. You can ask him.

c Complete the chart.

past simple: *be*	
present	past
I'm at home.	I ¹_____ at home.
You **aren't** at home.	You ²_____ at home.
Are you alone?	³_____ you alone?
No, I'm not.	No, I ⁴_____.

d 🅖p.110 **Grammar Bank 10B**

e 🔊10.13 Listen and say the sentences in the past.

> 1 ⟩⟩ *She's a teacher.* (*She was a teacher.*

2 LISTENING

a 🔊10.14 Listen to the detective interviewing Jason's friend, Kevin. Complete the information.

> Name: Kevin Smith
> Job: ¹_____
> Address: ²_____ Market Street
> Kevin knows Jason because they were ³_____ _____ together.
> At 5.00 yesterday afternoon, he was in his ⁴_____.
> At 7.00, he was in The ⁵_____ _____ pub in South ⁶_____.
> He was with Jason. His ⁷_____ and ⁸_____ _____ were there, too.

b Listen again. Why does the detective think that Kevin's story isn't true?

3 VOCABULARY *in, on, at*

a Look at Kevin and Jason's answers. What are the missing words?

> 1 Where were you yesterday afternoon at five o'clock?
>   I was _____ my taxi.
> 2 Where were you at seven o'clock last night?
>   I was _____ home.

b Complete the chart with *in, on,* or *at*.

Where were you yesterday at 7.00 p.m.?			
I was	¹_____	²_____	³_____
	home work school university	bed the kitchen my car London the park the street a restaurant a pub a museum a shopping centre a hotel	a bus a train a plane

c 🔊10.15 Listen and check. Repeat the sentences.

d Test a partner. **A** (book open) say a place. **B** (book closed) say the phrase. Then change.

> *the kitchen*) (*in the kitchen*

e ◀)) **10.16** The next day, Jason and Kevin were in prison. But where was Jason's wife? Listen and complete the sentences.

1 At 6.00, *she was in bed*.

2 At 8.00, _____ .

3 At 11.00, _____ .

4 At 3.00, _____ .

5 At 5.00, _____ .

6 At 7.00, _____ .

7 At 11.00, _____ again!

4 PRONUNCIATION & SPEAKING *was* and *were*, sentence rhythm

a ◀)) **10.17** Listen and repeat the conversation. C̲opy the rhy̲thm.

A **Where** were you at s̲even o'clock y̲esterday morning?
B I was at **home**.
A Were you in **bed**?
B **Yes**, I **was**.
A **Where** were you at **ten o'clock**?
B I was in a c̲afé with **friends**.
A Were you **there** all **morning**?
B **No**, we **weren't**. We were **there** for an **hour**.

b With a partner, ask and answer the questions.

1 Where were you yesterday at [7:00 AM] / [10:00 AM] in the morning?

2 Where were you yesterday at [4:00 PM] / [6:30 PM] in the afternoon?

3 Where were you at [9:30 PM] / [11:30 PM] last night?

4 Where were you last [Friday] / [Saturday] night?

5 ▶ VIDEO LISTENING Buildings with a past

a Watch the video *Buildings with a past*. Where are the buildings? What are they today? What were they in 1808?

> **Glossary**
> **cellar** an underground part of a house
> **vault** a room with strong walls for keeping money, e.g. in a bank

b Watch again. Mark the sentences **T** (true) or **F** (false).

1 The buildings are in the High Street, from number 92 to 94.
2 In the 15th century, they were part of Christ Church College.
3 In the 18th century, they were offices.
4 The buildings were a bank for about 200 years.
5 The hotel has 24 bedrooms.
6 The secret rooms are in the cellar.
7 The secret rooms were for keeping prisoners.
8 The doors were very difficult to open.
9 Today the rooms are for keeping wine.

c Would y̲ou like to stay at the hotel? Why (not)?

WORDS AND PHRASES TO LEARN 10B

p.132 Listen and repeat the words and phrases.

GRAMMAR

Circle a or b.

_____'s your name?
a Who   b What

1 Are you _____ at the moment?
   a work   b working

2 She _____ staying in a very good hotel.
   a isn't   b doesn't

3 He _____ his homework now.
   a doing   b is doing

4 A _____ raining?
   B No, it isn't.
   a Is it   b It's

5 Can you talk now, or _____?
   a are you driving   b do you drive

6 _____ to work by train?
   a Do you usually go
   b Are you usually going

7 I usually wear trousers, but today _____ a skirt.
   a I wear   b I'm wearing

8 _____ two beds in the room.
   a There is   b There are

9 There aren't _____ windows.
   a some   b any

10 _____ any towels in the bathroom?
   a Are there   b There are

11 Is there a swimming pool? Yes, _____.
   a there's   b there is

12 It _____ very hot last summer.
   a was   b were

13 Where _____ you yesterday at six o'clock?
   a was   b were

14 Karen _____ at school yesterday.
   a wasn't   b not was

15 _____ at home last night?
   a They were   b Were they

VOCABULARY

a Complete the phrases with a verb from the list.

arriving   carrying   phoning   ~~staying~~   waiting   wearing

   We're _staying_ in a beautiful hotel in the mountains.
1 A What are you doing here?
   B I'm _____ for my girlfriend. She's late.
2 A Who are you _____?   B My mother. It's her birthday.
3 Go and help that woman. She's _____ a very big suitcase.
4 Look! The train's _____. Can you see it?
5 Why are you _____ sunglasses? It's 11.00 in the evening!

b Write the clothes.

shoes   1 _____   2 _____   3 _____

4 _____   5 _____   6 _____   7 _____

c Complete the words.

   Would you like to have dinner in the hotel r_estaurant_?
1 When you arrive at a hotel you go to R_____ to check in.
2 You're in room 1122. Take the l_____ to the 11th floor.
3 I want to buy some presents. Is there a g_____ sh_____?
4 The b_____'s small. There's a shower, but there isn't a bath.
5 You can leave your car in the hotel c_____ p_____.

d Look at the picture. Complete the sentences with in, on, or under.

   The book is _on_ the chair.
1 The suitcase is _____ the bed.
2 The laptop is _____ the bed.
3 The lamps are _____ the tables.
4 The boots are _____ the chair.
5 The suitcases are _____ the cupboard.

e Complete with at, in, or on.

   Oh no! The keys are _in_ my car.
1 A Where's your mother?   B I think she's _____ the kitchen.
2 A Mike? It's Tim.   B Sorry, I can't hear you. I'm _____ a train.
3 A Is John here today?
   B No, he's _____ home. One of his children isn't well.

PRONUNCIATION

a Write the words for the sound pictures.

 *bike*

3

1

4

2

5

b 🅟 **p.134–5 Sound Bank** Look at more words with the sounds in **a**, and these sounds:

Practise saying the example words.

c <u>Under</u>line the stressed syllable.

<u>swea</u>|ter   2 a|rrive   4 cup|board

1 tra|vel   3 res|taurant   5 re|cep|tion

CAN YOU understand this text?

a Jenna and Max are going to Barcelona for the weekend. Read Jenna's tweets and number them 1–6.

A Our first dinner! 🙂 We're having amazing tapas in a bar in the old town, near the hotel. I love the 'pa amb tomàquet' (bread with tomatoes) and the Spanish ham.

B Our last morning! I don't want to go home! 🙁 Perhaps I can get a job in Barcelona?

C We're now at the hotel. Our room's great. There's a balcony and a view of the cathedral! I'm taking photos of everything for my blog.

D We're in the Picasso museum, looking at some of his early paintings. I love them! Then we're going to the beach for lunch! ☀

E The tapas were great. We're now lying on our bed watching a football match – Barcelona and Real Madrid! Come on, Barça! But Max prefers Madrid…

F We're waiting for the taxi to arrive and feeling a bit nervous! Our flight's at 16.30. Please hurry, taxi driver! Barcelona, here we come!

b Match the photos to the highlighted phrases in the tweets.

▶ CAN YOU understand these people?

🔊 **10.19** Watch or listen and answer the questions.

| 1 | 2 | 3 | 4 | 5 |
| Anna | Iain | Jayna | Sandra | Spencer |

1 Today Anna is _____ in Oxford.
   a seeing a friend
   b visiting a museum
   c doing some work
2 Iain usually wears _____ for work
   a a suit and tie
   b trousers and a jacket
   c trousers and a shirt
3 Jayna would like to live in England because she likes _____.
   a its people
   b its weather
   c its history
4 Sandra's hotel is _____.
   a quite expensive
   b in a nice place
   c in the city centre
5 Last night at 10 o'clock Spencer was _____.
   a at home
   b in a hotel
   c in a pub

CAN YOU say this in English?

Tick (✓) the boxes.

Can you…?	Yes, I can.
1 talk about what you're doing now	
2 say what you're wearing	
3 say what you would like to do	
4 identify things in a hotel room	
5 ask about facilities in a hotel	
6 say where you were yesterday, last night, etc.	

🔍 **Go online** to watch the video, review Files 9 & 10, and check your progress

G past simple: regular verbs   **V** regular verbs   **P** regular past simple endings

Did you decide to go to the USA?

Yes, we did. We wanted to live abroad.

1 GRAMMAR past simple: regular verbs

a 🔊 **11.1 Read and listen to Dominic. Choose a or b.**

1 Dominic and his wife wanted to live _____.
  a in another country   **b** in another place in their country
2 Duke University offered _____ a job in the USA.
  a Dominic   **b** Miriam
3 In the beginning, they _____ sure if they wanted to go.
  a were   **b** weren't

b 🔊 **11.2 Listen and match the sentences to photos A–F.**

1 ☐ We rented a house near the university.
2 ☐ We booked our flights. It was a long journey!
3 ☐ We invited our friends to our local pub to say goodbye.
4 ☐ We packed seven heavy suitcases.
5 ☐ The children didn't want to sleep on the plane. Sacha played with Lego and Elena looked at books.
6 ☐ When we arrived in North Carolina, we were very tired!

We followed our dream

My wife and I always wanted to live abroad. But Miriam and I both work in the UK – she's a doctor and I'm a designer – and we have two small children, Sacha and Elena. Then an American university, Duke, in Durham, North Carolina, asked Miriam to go and work there for a year. At first, we weren't sure what to do. There were so many questions. What about Sacha's school? What do we do with our house? But finally, we decided to go!

c Look at the highlighted verbs in sentences 1–6 and complete the chart. What letters do you add to the verb to make the positive ⊞ past form? How do you make the negative ⊟?

past simple: regular verbs	
present	past
we book	We _____ our flights.
we arrive	We _____ in North Carolina.
they don't want	They _____ want to sleep.

e In pairs, ask and answer questions with *Did...?* about the story in **a** and **b**. Answer *Yes, he / she / it / they did.* **OR** *No, he / she / it / they didn't.*

1 / Dominic and Miriam want to live abroad?
2 / Duke University offer Dominic a job?
3 / they invite their friends to their house?
4 / the children want to sleep on the plane?
5 / Sacha play with Lego on the plane?
6 / Elena play with Sacha?

Did Dominic and Miriam want to live abroad?

Yes, they did.

d 🅖 p.112 **Grammar Bank 11A**

2 PRONUNCIATION regular past simple endings

a 🔊 11.4 Listen and repeat the sounds and sentences.

🐕 **d**	**d**og	We arriv**ed** in North Carolina. Sacha play**ed** with Lego.
👕 **t**	**t**ie	We book**ed** our flights. Elena look**ed** at books. We pack**ed** seven heavy suitcases.
/ɪd/		We rent**ed** a house near the university. We invit**ed** our friends to our local pub.

b 🔊 11.5 Listen and repeat the sentences in **1b**.

c Cover the sentences. Look at photo A and say the sentence. Do the same for photos B–F.

3 SPEAKING

a Work with a partner.

A Make ⊞ or ⊟ true sentences about you with the phrases below. Add more information.

B Tick (✓) the things your partner did and cross (✗) the things he or she didn't do.

this morning	listen to the radio
	walk to work / school
	arrive late at work / school
last night	phone a friend
	watch TV
	study English
last weekend	play a sport or game
	cook lunch or dinner
	help in the house

(I listened to the radio this morning in the car.
  (I didn't walk to work.

b Change roles.

c Work with a new partner. Ask and answer about his or her old partner.

Did Anna listen to the radio this morning?)
  (Yes, she did. She listened to it in the car.
Did she walk to work?) (No, she didn't.

4 READING & LISTENING

a 🔊 11.6 Read and listen to part of Dominic's blog about their life in the USA. What did they like about the USA? What was a problem for them?

Sacha at school

We want to go back to _____!

At first living in the USA was quite difficult. We missed our friends and family and we didn't like the food. It was difficult to find organic fruit and vegetables. We also needed to rent a car. In London, we don't drive, but in Durham, not many people walk or use public transport!

But we soon started to enjoy it. Our house was nice, and near a lovely park. Sacha liked his school, especially his music teacher, who played the trumpet! He worked hard and his teachers were very happy with him.

b 🔊 11.7 Listen to the rest of the blog. Complete the title in **a** with *the UK* or *the USA*.

A trip to a blueberry farm

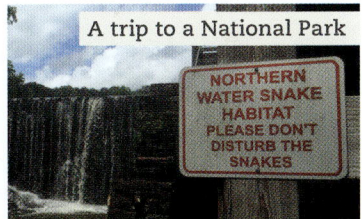
A trip to a National Park

c Listen again and correct the information.
1 Miriam wasn't very happy at work.
2 Dominic worked in an office.
3 Life in the USA was very expensive.
4 The children learned to play tennis.
5 The people in Durham weren't very friendly.
6 The National Parks were similar to English parks.
7 At the blueberry farm they listened to classical music.
8 They stayed in Durham for two years.
9 They returned to England because they missed their life there.

d Do you know anyone who lived or studied in another country? Where were they? Was it a good experience?

WORDS AND PHRASES TO LEARN 11A

p.132 Listen and repeat the words and phrases.

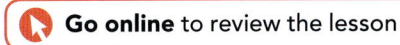
🔵 **Go online** to review the lesson

Did you have a good day?

Yes, I had a great day.

1 VOCABULARY verb phrases with *get, go, have, do*

a Complete the verb phrases.

to bed   breakfast   a coffee   dinner   a~~flight~~   home
homework   housework   lunch   a nice day   out
to school   a shower   sport   a~~taxi~~   ~~up~~~~early~~   yoga

a flight

up early   **get**   a taxi

have

b 🔊 **11.9** Listen and check.

c Test a partner. **A** (book open) say a phrase from the list.
B (book closed) say the phrase with the correct verb.

a flight ⟩ ⟨ *get a flight*

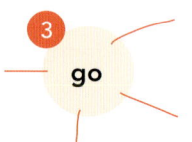

go

do

2 LISTENING

a 🔊 **11.10** Ben was in Paris for the day on business.
He arrived home in London at 4.00 p.m. Listen to
the conversation with his daughter, Linda. Tick (✓)
the places where she says she was during the day.

☐ at home   ☐ in a restaurant
☐ in a museum   ☐ in a café
☐ in a shopping centre   ☐ at school

b Listen again and read the conversation. Complete
the missing words.

c 🔊 **11.11** What do <u>you</u> think the noise is? Listen
and check.

3 GRAMMAR past simple irregular verbs: *get, go, have, do*

a Read the conversation in **2b** again. Complete the
chart.

present simple	past simple
I get	I _____ an early flight.
We go	We _____ to the British Museum.
We have	We _____ lunch in the café.
I do	I _____ my homework.

b 🔊 **11.12** Listen and check. Then repeat the past
simple sentences.

c **G** p.112 Grammar Bank 11B

B Hi. I'm back. Linda! What are you doing at ¹h_____?
L Hi, Dad. You're very early.
B Yes, I got an early ²fl_____.
L How was your day?
B My day was fine. But what about your day? Why aren't
you at school?
L We didn't have ³cl_____ today. We went to the
⁴Br_____ Museum in the morning. It was great.
And then we had ⁵l_____ in the café there.
B Why didn't you go to school this afternoon?
L We had a ⁶fr_____ afternoon. I stayed at home.
B What did you do?
L I did my ⁷h_____. I had a lot of work.
B Good girl. When are your exams?
L They're next ⁸w_____.
B Where's your ⁹m_____?
L She went out. I think she went ¹⁰sh_____.
B What's that?
L What?
B That noise.

4 PRONUNCIATION & SPEAKING
sentence rhythm

a 🔊 **11.14** Listen and repeat the questions and answers. <u>Copy</u> the <u>rhy</u>thm.

> A **What time** did you **get up**?
> B I **got up** at **7.30**.
> A Did you **have breakfast**?
> B **Yes**, I **did**.
> A **What** did you **have**?
> B I **had toast** and **coffee**.
> A **What** did you **do then**?
> B I **went** to **work**.

b Ⓒ **Communication** Your day **p.81** Interview a partner about yesterday.

5 READING

a *Life in a Day* is a film produced by Ridley Scott. Read the introduction to the article. What did a lot of people do on 24th July?

b 🔊 **11.15** Look at the photos with the article. Read and listen to the rest of the article. Complete captions 1–5.

c Read the article again. Then answer the questions with a partner.
1 What normal things did people do on 24th July?
2 What unusual things did they do?

d Cover the article. Can you remember the past tense of these verbs?

do   get up   go   have   open   wash   work

e Complete the sentences with a verb from **d**.
1 The children _____ at 7.45 this morning and they were late for school.
2 I was very happy when I _____ my birthday present. It was exactly what I wanted!
3 I _____ my English homework on the bus yesterday.
4 I _____ very hard today. I'm really tired!
5 Last summer we _____ to France on holiday. We were very lucky – we _____ fantastic weather.
6 A Is this a new car?
    B No, it's two years old, but I _____ it this morning!

6 WRITING

Ⓦ **p.87 Writing** A blog post Write about what you did yesterday.

WORDS AND PHRASES TO LEARN 11B

p.132 Listen and repeat the words and phrases.

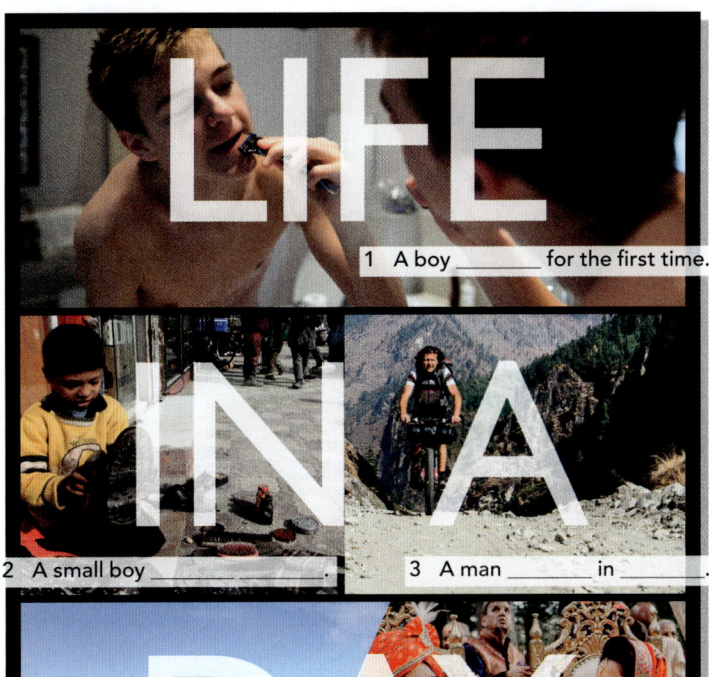

LIFE IN A DAY

1 A boy _____ for the first time.
2 A small boy _____ .
3 A man _____ in _____ .
4 A woman _____ a _____ .
5 A man and a woman _____ .

WE ASKED PEOPLE AROUND THE WORLD TO FILM THEIR LIVES. WE GOT 4,500 HOURS OF VIDEO FROM 102 COUNTRIES. ALL OF IT WAS FILMED ON THE SAME DAY – 24TH JULY.

Early in the morning in the USA, a baby opened his eyes and looked at his mother. 'Isn't he pretty?' she asked the camera. Around the world, people got up, and washed, and had breakfast. A 15-year-old boy shaved for the first time. He didn't enjoy it! A small boy kissed his mother on her birthday.

24th of July was a Saturday, so a lot of people didn't go to work. They relaxed and went to the park with their family, or went shopping. But other people worked hard, or cooked and cleaned. Some children played – but others worked. One small boy cleaned shoes in the street. One woman went to hospital for an operation. Another woman waited all evening to talk to her husband on Skype. He was a soldier thousands of miles from home.

For some people, 24th of July was a special day. A man arrived in Kathmandu. He was on a cycle trip around the world. A woman did an incredible skydive. An unemployed man got his first job. A boy who was at university went home to see his father for the first time in three years. Another man asked his girlfriend to marry him. A man and a woman got married and had an incredible party.

This beautiful film shows us life around the world in the 21st century. Watch it! It's free on YouTube.

Go online to review the lesson

Practical English Is there a bank near

asking for and giving directions **V** prepositions of place **P** sentence rhythm and polite intonation

1 VOCABULARY & PRONUNCIATION
prepositions of place; sentence rhythm and polite intonation

a 🔊 **11.17** Listen and repeat the words and phrases.

1 next to   2 <u>o</u>pposite   3 be<u>tween</u>

4 on the <u>corner</u>   5 on the left   6 on the right

b 🔊 **11.18** Look at the map and the names of the streets and buildings. Listen and complete the places A–D.

coffee shop   Chinese restaurant   phone shop   park

c 🔊 **11.19** Listen and repeat the conversation. <u>Copy</u> the <u>rhythm</u> and polite intonation.

> A **Excuse** me. Is there a **bank near here**?
> B **Yes**, there's **one** on the **corner** of **King Street** and **East Road**.
> A **Thank you**.

d Practise in pairs. Choose places on the map.

Excuse me. Is there a...near here?

Yes, there's one on...

HOSPITAL

TRAIN STATION

A

HOTEL

EAST ROAD

NORTH STREET

LONDON ROAD

SCHOOL ROAD

CAR PARK

BANK

B

GYM

C

SCHOOL

FACTORY

ITALIAN RESTAURANT

CINEMA

D

SUPERMARKET

BOOKSHOP

KING STREET

SOUTH STREET

here?

2 ▶ ASKING FOR AND GIVING DIRECTIONS

a ◀)) **11.20** Match the words and pictures. Watch or listen and check. Watch or listen again and repeat.

A Turn right.   B Turn left.   C Go straight on.

b ◀)) **11.21** Rob needs to take out some money. He's looking for a cash machine. Watch or listen. Which bank does he go to, A, B, or C?

Rob is here.

Rob	Excuse me. Is there a cash machine near here?
Woman	Yes. There's one at Barclays Bank.
Rob	Sorry, where is that?
Woman	Turn left and go straight on. Then turn right and it's on the right.
Rob	Thanks very much.
Woman	You're welcome.

c In pairs, practise the conversation in **b**.

d ◀)) **11.22** The cash machine isn't working. Watch or listen to Rob asking for more directions. Which bank does he go to now?

e ⓒ**Communication** Excuse me. Can you help me? **A** p.81 **B** p.85 Practise asking for directions.

3 ▶ WHERE'S JENNY'S HOTEL?

a ◀)) **11.23** Watch or listen to Rob and Jenny on the phone. Why is he phoning her?

b Watch or listen again. Complete the information about Jenny's hotel.

Hotel ^{1} Indigo, ^{2}_____ Street. It's near Paddington ^{3}_____. Get the Heathrow Express train from the ^{4}_____ to Paddington. It only takes about ^{5}_____ minutes.

DIRECTIONS: Turn ^{6}_____ when you leave the station. Then go ^{7}_____ for a bit and turn ^{8}_____ into London Street. The hotel's ^{9}_____ Norfolk Square.

4 ▶ USEFUL PHRASES

◀)) **11.24** Watch or listen and repeat the useful phrases.

Is there a cash machine near here?
Thanks very much.
You're welcome.
I don't believe it!
Excuse me, this cash machine isn't working.
It only takes about 15 minutes.
Turn left when you leave the station.

Go online to watch the video and review the lesson

Where did he see her?

He saw her on the train.

| G past simple: regular and irregular verbs | V regular and irregular verbs | P irregular verbs |

1 VOCABULARY & PRONUNCIATION
regular and irregular verbs

a Do the Verbs quiz with a partner.

VERBS QUIZ

1 **Look at the regular verbs and answer the questions.**

arrive ask exchange finish look
move open phone start stop
talk wait

a Which verb doubles the final consonant before the -ed ending?
b Which four verbs only add -d?
c In which two verbs is the -ed ending pronounced /ɪd/?

2 **Match the past simple of the irregular verbs to the verbs.**

wrote bought sent sat
left said told saw

buy _____   send _____
leave _____   sit _____
say _____   tell _____
see _____   write _____

b ◀)) 12.1 Listen and repeat the verbs in the quiz in the past tense.

c ◀)) 12.2 Cover the quiz. Listen and say the verb in the past tense.

1)) say (said
2)) tell (told

2 READING & LISTENING

◀)) 12.3–12.4 Read and listen to the story. In pairs, ask and answer the questions after each part.

Strangers on a train

◀)) 12.3 **Part 1**

When the train stopped at the station, I opened my eyes and looked out of the window. I saw a woman on the platform. She was tall and blonde with blue eyes. The train moved and I closed my eyes. It was 4.00 p.m. and the train was full.

'Excuse me. Can I sit here?' I opened my eyes again. It was the tall, blonde woman.

'Sure,' I answered. She sat down next to me. There was a nice smell. Chanel No. 5. I started to listen to music on my phone.

'I love Chopin.'

'Sorry?' I said.

'You're listening to Chopin. I love classical music.' She smiled. Her eyes were very blue.

We talked about music until the train arrived at Paddington Station. 'Would you like a cup of coffee?' she asked me. I looked at my watch. 'OK,' I said. 'I have time.'

1 Where did the man first see the woman?
2 What was the woman's perfume?
3 What did they talk about?
4 What did the woman invite him to do when the train arrived?

◀) 12.4 Part 2

We bought two coffees at the station café. We sat down.

'My name's Olivia,' she said.

'I'm David. I'm from Chicago. Nice to meet you. What do you do?' I asked.

'I work in property – flats and houses. What do you do?'

'I work for Citibank.'

'That's interesting!' said Olivia. 'Do you live in London?'

'Yes, but I'm new here. I moved to London last month. I have a flat in Chelsea.'

'Wow! That's an expensive part of London!'

I looked at my watch. 'Time to go. I have a tennis lesson this evening.'

'I can drive you home,' she said. 'I live near Chelsea.' I told her my address.

5 What's Olivia's job?
6 What's David's job?
7 Where do they live?
8 Why did David give Olivia his address?

3 GRAMMAR past simple: regular and irregular verbs

a Read the conversations and circle the correct form.

1 A Where did you **go / went** on Saturday?
   B I **go / went** shopping for clothes.
   A What did you **buy / bought**?
   B I **buy / bought** a new jacket.
   A **Did / Was** it expensive?
   B No, it **didn't / wasn't**.

2 A What **did you do / did you** last night?
   B I **was / went** to the cinema. I **see / saw** a new French film.
   A **Did / Was** you **like / liked** it?
   B No, I **didn't like / didn't liked** it very much. It **was / were** very slow.

b ◀) 12.5 Listen and check.

c Ⓖ p.114 Grammar Bank 12A

d With a partner, retell Parts 1 and 2 of the story. Use the questions to help you.
• How did David meet Olivia?
• What did they talk about?
• What happened at Paddington Station?
• How did David get home from the station?

4 ▶ VIDEO LISTENING
Strangers on a train

a ◀) 12.9 Watch or listen to *Strangers on a train* Part 3. Answer the questions.
1 What kind of car did Olivia have?
2 What did she have two tickets for?
3 Where did she want to meet him? What time?

b ◀) 12.10 Watch or listen to *Strangers on a train* Part 4. Answer the questions.
1 What time did David arrive at the concert hall?
2 What happened at 7.45? What did David do?
3 What did David do when the concert finished?
4 What did he do after that?
5 Why do you think Olivia didn't come to the concert?
6 What do you think David saw when he opened the door?

c ◀) 12.11 Watch or listen to Part 5, the end of the story. Do you think it was a good ending?

WORDS AND PHRASES TO LEARN 12A

p.132 Listen and repeat the words and phrases.

Ⓖ **Go online** to review the lesson

G past simple revision **V** revision of past verb forms **P** revision of vowel sounds

> What did you do last Saturday?

> I went to the country.

Play the game in groups of three or four.

1 Say five things you did yesterday morning.

2 What did you do for your last summer holiday?

3 Ask your group three questions with *Where were you yesterday at...?*

4 *be, have,* or *do*? Which verb do we use with each expression?

_____ a good day _____ tired _____ sport
_____ hungry _____ homework _____ lunch

Make three ⊞ or ⊟ sentences about yesterday with three different phrases.

15 Which verb has a different vowel sound?

painted rained said waited

Make a sentence with each verb.

14 Which verb is irregular? What's its past form?

book go pack stay

Make two ⊞ or ⊟ sentences about your last holiday with two different verbs.

13 What was the last film you saw? When and where did you see it? Did you like it?

12 Did you go shopping last week? Where? What did you buy?

16 What time did you get up this morning? Were you tired?

17 When is your birthday? What did you do on your last birthday?

18 When was the last time you talked to a stranger? What did you talk about?

19 Complete the verb in each phrase. What's the past tense of each verb?

b_____ new clothes
s_____ 'sorry' to somebody
s_____ a film

When was the last time you did each thing?

30 Which verb has a different vowel sound?

bought saw talked worked

Make two sentences about last Friday with two different verbs.

29 Complete the verb in each phrase. What's the past tense of each verb?

s_____ a message
u_____ a laptop
wr_____ an email

When was the last time you did each thing?

28 Choose a day last week. Ask your group three questions with *On _____day, did you...?*

27 Did you do any sport or exercise last week? What did you do?

5

In which verb(s) is the *-ed* ending pronounced /ɪd/?

hat**ed**   lik**ed**   lov**ed**   want**ed**

Make two sentences about when you were a child with two different verbs.

6

What did you have for breakfast this morning? Where did you have it?

7

What's the last big city you visited?

8

When was the last time you bought a souvenir? What was it?

11

What did you do last Saturday?

10

In which verb(s) is the *-ed* ending pronounced /ɪd/?

decid**ed**   need**ed**   open**ed**   watch**ed**

Make two sentences about last night with two different verbs.

9

Complete the verb in each phrase. Make a ＋ or － sentence about yesterday with each verb.

d_____ housework
g_____ up in the morning
h_____ a nice evening
w_____ for a bus

20

Match a verb from 1 to one with the same vowel sound in 2.

1 ch**a**nged   **a**nswered   rel**a**xed
2 tr**a**velled   p**a**rked   pl**a**yed

Choose one pair of verbs. Make two sentences.

21

Did you get a bus or a train last week? Where to?

22

How many hours of TV did you watch yesterday? What programmes?

23

How did you come to class today? Were you late?

26

Where did you have lunch last Sunday? Who with?

25

Which verb has a different vowel sound?

did   liked   listened   lived

Make a sentence with each verb.

24

Which verb <u>can't</u> you use with the **bold** noun?

cook / drink / have   **dinner**
eat / have / want   **a coffee**
buy / travel / want   **new shoes**

Make positive ＋ or negative － sentences about last week with three of the phrases.

🖱 **Go online** to review the lesson

GRAMMAR

Circle a or b.

_____'s your name?
a Who b **What**

1 They _____ English at school.
   a studied b studied

2 _____ the film?
   a Did you like b Liked you

3 He _____ late yesterday.
   a doesn't work b didn't work

4 What time _____?
   a did they arrive b did they arrived

5 I _____ to the USA last year.
   a was b went

6 I _____ the homework last night.
   a didn't do b didn't

7 What time did you _____ this morning?
   a get up b got up

8 We _____ lunch at a great restaurant on Sunday.
   a haved b had

9 Where _____ on holiday?
   a did you go b you did go

10 A _____ the film good?
   B Yes, fantastic.
   a Did b Was

11 I liked the jacket, but I _____ it.
   a didn't buy b didn't bought

12 A What time _____ to bed last night?
   B At 10.15.
   a did you went b did you go

13 Alice _____ to Dublin last month.
   a goes b went

14 Maria _____ to class yesterday.
   a didn't come b didn't came

15 What time _____?
   a finished the concert
   b did the concert finish

VOCABULARY

a Write the words or phrases.

opposite   1 _____   2 _____

3 _____ the _____   4 _____ the _____   5 _____ the _____

b Write the past tense of the verbs (regular or irregular).

ask _asked_	help _____	sit _____
buy _____	leave _____	start _____
carry _____	miss _____	stay _____
change _____	need _____	study _____
cry _____	open _____	talk _____
do _____	say _____	tell _____
have _____	send _____	write _____

PRONUNCIATION

a Write the words for the sound pictures.

bike   3 _____

1 _____   4 _____

2 _____   5 _____

b ℗ p.134–5 Sound Bank Look at more words with the sounds in **a**, and these sounds:

Practise saying the example words.

c Underline the stressed syllable.

wea|ther   2 be|tween   4 u|ni|ver|si|ty
1 o|ppo|site   3 de|cide   5 ex|change

CAN YOU understand this text?

A Unique Culture

I studied for three months at Al-Ahliyya Amman University, in Amman, the capital of Jordan. It was a life-changing experience. Every day was a new adventure – very different from my life in the USA. While I was there, I studied US politics in the Middle East, the history of the Arab World, and Arabic language.

People often ask me what my favourite memory is, but it's difficult to answer because there are so many! I loved riding a camel in the Wadi Rum desert and I went on an amazing excursion to Petra. The countryside was beautiful and completely different from where I live in the United States. I also enjoyed the unique culture of Jordan. Of course, there were things that I sometimes found difficult, but everybody from Jordan was very understanding and friendly.

My recommendation for people who want to study abroad is to go to a country that is completely different from where you live and to stay as long as you can. I loved learning about another culture and I think studying abroad is a great experience.

The ancient city of Petra

a Read the article about Delaney Morgan, an American student who studied in Jordan. Which three places in Jordan does she mention?

b Read again and mark the sentences **T** (true) or **F** (false).

1 Delaney spent three weeks in Jordan.
2 Her life there was different from her life at home.
3 She didn't learn any Arabic.
4 She has a lot of good memories of Jordan.
5 She stayed in Amman all the time.
6 She didn't like the countryside.
7 The Jordanians weren't always very friendly.
8 She thinks it's good to experience life in another country.

▶ CAN YOU understand these people?

◀) **12.13** Watch or listen and answer the questions.

1	2	3	4	5
Sophie	Jayna	Rozie	Chimi	Susan

1 Last weekend it ____.
   a was nice weather
   b was Sophie's friend's birthday
   c rained
2 For her last holiday Jayna went to ____.
   a Germany
   b Japan
   c Jamaica
3 Rozie had a good meal recently at a ____.
   a French restaurant
   b Mexican restaurant
   c Chinese restaurant
4 Chimi isn't very good at ____ directions.
   a understanding
   b giving
   c understanding or giving
5 Susan says there's a café ____.
   a on the right
   b on the left
   c on the corner

CAN YOU say this in English?

Tick (✓) the boxes.

Can you...?	Yes, I can.
1 say what you did yesterday, last weekend, etc.	☐
2 ask for and give directions in a town	☐
3 ask questions about the past	☐

Communication

1B WHERE IS IT? Student A

a   Ask **B** questions for your cities.

Where's Izmir?

1 **Izmir** is in Turkey.
2 **Atlanta** is in the United States.
3 **Basel** is in Switzerland.
4 **Curitiba** is in Brazil.
5 **Dortmund** is in Germany.
6 **Gdansk** is in Poland.
7 **Hong Kong** is in China.
8 **Luxor** is in Egypt.

b   Answer **B**'s questions with a country.

It's in… *I think it's in…* *I don't know.*

← p.8

PE1 HIT THE SHIPS Student A

a   Draw five 'ships' in **Your ships**.

Your ships

	1	2	3	4	5	6	7	8	9	10
A										
B										
C										
D										
E										
F										
G										
H										
I										
J										

One ship = three squares

B's ships

	1	2	3	4	5	6	7	8	9	10
A										
B										
C										
D										
E										
F										
G										
H										
I										
J										

b   Try to 'hit' **B**'s ships. Say a square, e.g. *H8*. If **B** says *Hit*, tick (✓) the square in **B**'s ships. If **B** says *Nothing*, cross (✗) the square.

H8? *Nothing.*   *B7?* *Hit!*

c   **B** says a square. Say *Hit* or *Nothing*.

← p.10

2A IS SUSHI CHINESE? Student A

1 _____ sushi Chinese?

6 Gisele Bündchen is Brazilian.

2 _____ the Rolling Stones American?

7 Lada cars are Russian.

3 _____ Giorgio Armani Italian?

8 Tacos are Mexican.

4 _____ Victoria Beckham Australian?

9 Antonio Banderas is Spanish.

5 _____ the pyramids Egyptian?

10 Swatch and Rolex are Swiss.

a   Ask **B** about 1–5. Use *Is…?* or *Are…?* Tick (✓) if the answer is yes. If the answer is no, write the nationality.

Is sushi Chinese?

b   Answer **B**'s question about 6–10.

No, he / she / it isn't. He / She / It's…
Yes, they are.
No, they aren't. They're…

← p.13

2B PERSONAL INFORMATION Student A

a Interview **B** and complete **B**'s form.

What's your first name?) (*Chris.*

How do you spell it?) (*C-H-R-I-S.*

Student B	
First name	
Surname	
Nationality	
Address	
Postcode	
Age	
Married ☐ Single ☐	
Phone number	home
	mobile
Email address	

b Answer **B**'s questions. Use the information in the **YOU** form.

YOU	
First name	Alex
Surname	Barrett
Nationality	British
Address	15 Park Road, York
Postcode	YO6 4PX
Age	25
Married ☐ Single ✔	
Phone number	home 0113 496 0752
	mobile 07700 900528
Email address	abarrett65@bt.com

◀ p.15

3B HOW MUCH ARE THESE WATCHES? Student A

a Look at your picture. You are a customer. Ask **B** about the missing prices. Use *this / that* for singular objects **OR** *these / those* for plural objects. Write the prices.

How much is this mug?) (*It's…*

b Now **B** is a customer. Answer **B**'s questions with a price.

(*It's / They're…pounds.*

◀ p.21

PE3 WHAT TIME IS IT? Student A

a Ask **B** a question to complete the time on clock 1.

(*Clock 1: What time is it?*

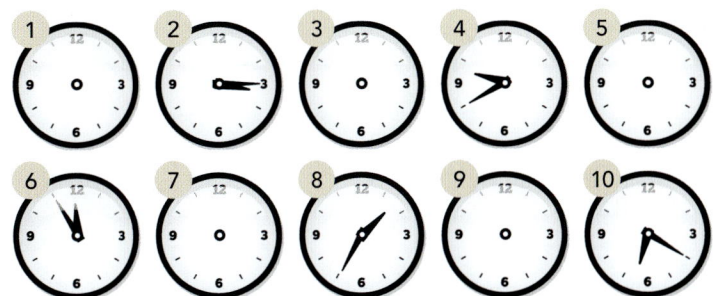

b Answer **B**'s question about clock 2.

(*It's…*

c Continue with the other clocks.　　◀ p.34

8A I'M A TOURIST. WHERE CAN I...?
Student A

a You are a tourist. **B** lives in this town. Ask **B** your questions.

In this town

where can I...?
- have a good, cheap meal
- see films in English
- go with small children
- go in the evening

Can I...?
- take photos in museums
- drive in the town centre

b You live in this town. Answer **B**'s questions about your town, or a town you know well. ← p.49

9A THE SAME OR DIFFERENT? Student A

a Say what the woman in picture 1 is doing. **B** says if his / her picture is the same or different. Write **S** or **D**.

b Now listen to **B** describe the person in picture 2. Is your person the same or different? Write **S** or **D**.

c Continue with people 3–8.

d Compare your pictures and check your answers.

← p.55

10A IS THERE A TV? WHERE IS IT?
Student A

a Look at picture 1. Ask **B** questions about the things in the list for the picture.

books coat Cokes keys lamp laptop newspaper suitcase towels TV

Are there any books? *Is there a coat?*

If **B** answers *Yes*, ask *Where are they?* **OR** *Where is it?* Draw the thing(s) in the correct places in picture 1.

b Look at picture 2 and answer **B**'s questions.

← p.61

11B YOUR DAY Students A+B

a What did you do yesterday? Ask and answer the questions with a partner. Write your partner's answers.

What time did you get up yesterday?

I got up at 6.30 in the morning.

YOUR DAY	Your partner
1 What time / get up yesterday?	
2 / have a shower?	
3 / have breakfast? What / have?	
4 / go to work or school? How / get there?	
5 What time / start work or school?	
6 Where / have lunch? / enjoy it?	
7 What time / go home?	
8 / do homework or housework?	
9 What / have for dinner?	
10 / watch TV? What / watch?	
11 What time / go to bed?	
12 / have a good day?	

b Change partners. Tell your new partner three things about your first partner.

 p.69

PE6 EXCUSE ME. CAN YOU HELP ME?
Student A

a Ask **B** for directions to the bus station. Then mark it on the map (building 1, 2, or 3). You begin:

Excuse me. Can you help me? Where's the bus station, please?

b Help **B** when he / she asks you for directions to the university.

Excuse me. … *Go…*

c Now ask **B** for directions to the Park Hotel and the phone shop. Then mark them on the map.

d Give **B** directions to the sports centre and the shoe factory.

 p.71

3A MEMORY GAME Students A+B

a Look at the photo for 30 seconds.

b Close your book. In pairs, can you remember all the things?

A watch. *No, two watches, I think.* p.18

1B WHERE IS IT? Student B

a Answer **A**'s questions with a country.

(*It's in…* (*I think it's in…* (*I don't know.*

b Ask **A** questions for your cities.

(*Where's Acapulco?*

1 **Acapulco** is in Mexico.
2 **Las Vegas** is in the United States.
3 **Manchester** is in England.
4 **Milan** is in Italy
5 **Osaka** is in Japan.
6 **Rostov** is in Russia.
7 **Toulouse** is in France.
8 **Valencia** is in Spain.

 p.8

PE1 HIT THE SHIPS Student B

a Draw five 'ships' in **Your ships**.

Your ships

	1	2	3	4	5	6	7	8	9	10
A										
B										
C										
D										
E										
F										
G										
H										
I										
J										

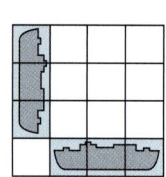

One ship
= three
squares

A's ships

	1	2	3	4	5	6	7	8	9	10
A										
B										
C										
D										
E										
F										
G										
H										
I										
J										

b **A** says a square, e.g. *H8*. If you have a ship in H8, say *Hit*. If not, say *Nothing*.

H8?) (*Nothing.* *B7?*) (*Hit!*

c Try to 'hit' **A**'s ships. Say a square, e.g. *B3*. If **A** says *Hit*, tick (✓) the square in **A**'s ships. If **A** says *Nothing*, cross (✗) the square.

 p.10

2A IS SUSHI CHINESE? Student B

Sushi is Japanese.

_____ Gisele Bündchen German?

The Rolling Stones are British.

_____ Lada cars Polish?

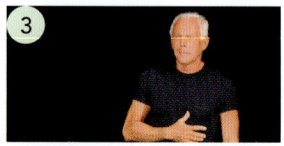
Giorgio Armani is Italian.

_____ tacos Mexican?

Victoria Beckham is British.

_____ Antonio Banderas Italian?

The Pyramids are Egyptian.

_____ Swatch and Rolex Swiss?

a Answer **A**'s question about 1–5.

Yes, he / she / it is.)
No, he / she / it isn't. He / She / It's…)
Yes, they are.)
No, they aren't. They're…)

b Ask **A** about 6–10. Use *Is…?* or *Are…?* Tick (✓) if the answer is yes. If the answer is no, write the nationality.

(*Is Gisele Bündchen German?*

p.13

2B PERSONAL INFORMATION Student B

a Answer **A**'s questions. Use the information in the **YOU** form.

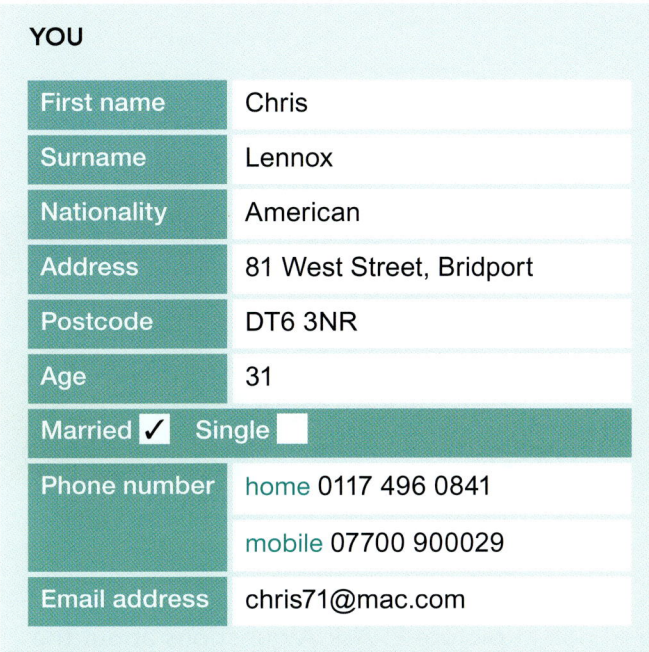

YOU	
First name	Chris
Surname	Lennox
Nationality	American
Address	81 West Street, Bridport
Postcode	DT6 3NR
Age	31
Married ✓ Single ☐	
Phone number	home 0117 496 0841
	mobile 07700 900029
Email address	chris71@mac.com

b Interview **A** and complete **A**'s form.

What's your first name? *Chris.*
How do you spell it? *C-H-R-I-S.*

Student A	
First name	
Surname	
Nationality	
Address	
Postcode	
Age	
Married ☐ Single ☐	
Phone number	home
	mobile
Email address	

⬅ p.15

3B HOW MUCH ARE THESE WATCHES? Student B

a Look at your picture. **A** is a customer. Answer **A**'s questions with a price.

It's / They're...pounds.

b Now you are a customer. Ask **A** about the missing prices. Use *this / these* **OR** *that / those*. Write the prices.

How much is this flag? *It's...*

⬅ p.21

PE3 WHAT TIME IS IT? Student B

a Answer **A**'s question about clock 1.

It's...

b Ask **A** a question to complete the time on clock 2.

Clock 2: What time is it?

c Continue with the other clocks.   ⬅ p.34

8A I'M A TOURIST. WHERE CAN I...?
Student B

a You live in this town. Answer **A**'s questions about your town, or a town you know well.

b You are a tourist. **A** lives in this town. Ask **A** your questions.

In this town

where can I...?
- go for a nice walk
- go shopping for souvenirs
- park near the town centre
- eat really good food

Can I...?
- go shopping on Sundays
- pay by credit card in bars and small shops

OPEN
MON – SAT
11 – 8PM
SUN
11 – 6PM

← p.49

9A THE SAME OR DIFFERENT? Student B

a Listen to **A** describe what the woman in picture 1 is doing. Is your person the same or different? Write **S** or **D**.

b Describe the person in picture 2 to **A**. Say what he / she is doing. **A** says if his / her picture is the same or different. Write **S** or **D**.

c Continue with people 3–8.

d Compare your pictures and check your answers.

10A IS THERE A TV? WHERE IS IT?
Student B

a Look at picture 1 and answer **A**'s questions.

b Look at picture 2. Ask **A** questions about the things below for the picture.

Is there a bag? *Are there any books?*

bag books clock Cokes extra pillows laptop
pens remote control towels TV

If **A** answers *Yes*, ask *Where is it?* **OR** *Where are they?* Draw the thing(s) in the correct places in picture 2.

← p.61

PE6 EXCUSE ME. CAN YOU HELP ME?
   Student B

a Help **A** when he / she asks you for directions to the bus station.

Excuse me. ... *Go...*

b Ask **A** for directions to the university. Then mark it on the map (building 1, 2, or 3). You begin:

Excuse me. Can you help me? Where's the university, please?

c Help **A** when he / she asks you for directions to the Park Hotel and the phone shop.

d Ask **A** for directions to the sports centre and the shoe factory. Then mark them on the map.

⬅ p.71

9B UNDERCOVER BOSS Students A+B

FRIDAY At the end of the week, David says to the workers: 'I'm not "Andy". I'm David Clarke, your boss.' The workers are very surprised. He tells them about his experience and asks them to make some changes. He also helps individual workers and gives the very good ones more money. David thinks going undercover is the only way to really discover what is happening in a company.

⬅ p.56

Writing

1 A FORM

a Look at the form. Match each part to a question a–h below.

- a [ ] Are you married?
- b [ ] What's your home phone number?
- c [ ] What's your postcode?
- d [ ] How old are you?
- e [ ] What's your email?
- f [1] What's your name?
- g [ ] What's your mobile number?
- h [ ] What's your address?

CREDIT CARD Application form

1 First name

Surname

Title: Mr ☐ Ms ☐ Mrs ☐

2 Age

3 Married ☐ Single ☐
Divorced / Separated ☐

4 Address

5 Postcode

6 Email

Phone number 7 home

8 mobile

b Complete the form for you. Tick (✓) your title, too.

> 🔍 **Titles**
> Mr = a man, Ms = a woman,
> Mrs = a married woman
>
> **Capital letters**
> **A**dam **D**avis **NOT** ~~adam davis~~
> 245 **G**reen **S**treet **NOT** ~~245 green street~~
> **L**ondon **NOT** ~~london~~

⬅ p.15

2 A POST ABOUT A PHOTO

a Read about Alice and her family. Write the numbers of the people on the photo.

My name is ¹Alice and I'**m** from Toulouse in France**.** This is a photo of my family. My father'**s** name is ²Henri**,** and my mother's name is ³Cécile. I have a sister, ⁴Pauline, and a brother, ⁵Olivier. We have a dog. His name is ⁶Toto. Do you like my photo**?**

b Look at the highlighted punctuation in the text and read the information box.

> 🔍 **Punctuation**
> full stop (.)   *My name is Alice and I'm from Toulouse.*
>   **NOT** *~~My name is Alice and I'm from Toulouse~~*
> comma (,)   *I have a sister, Pauline, and a brother, Olivier.*
> question mark (?) *Do you like my photo?*
> apostrophe (') *I'm from Toulouse.* **NOT** *~~Im from Toulouse.~~*
>   *My father's name…* **NOT** *~~My fathers name…~~*

c Post a photo of your family and write about it. ⬅ p.25

3 A COMMENT POST

a Read Marcos's comment. Do you like his breakfast?

> **LET'S CHAT! TODAY'S QUESTION:**
>
> Is breakfast important for you? What do you have? Where do you have it?
> _____
>
> **Marcos, Cuenca, Spain** *7 mins ago*
> Breakfast is very important for me! I have fruit, usually an orange **or** an apple.
> Then I have bread with butter **and** jam, and a cup of coffee.
> I usually have breakfast at home, **but** at the weekend I have it in a bar near my house. I think my breakfast is very healthy.

b Look at the highlighted words. Complete sentences 1–3 with *and*, *or*, or *but*.

1 I eat fish, _____ I don't eat meat.
2 Do you have tea _____ coffee for breakfast?
3 I have a brother _____ a sister.

c Write a comment about <u>your</u> breakfast. What do you have? Is it healthy? Use *and*, *but*, and *or* to connect. ⬅ p.31

4 AN EMAIL

a Read the email from Lucy. What does she invite Kate to?

> **From:** Lucy Lewis <LL1991@netlink.com>
> **To:** Kate <ksavage@topmail.net>
> **Subject:** Dinner
>
> Hi Kate,
>
> Would you like to come to dinner on Thursday? I'm inviting Moira and Jerry, too.
>
> Can you come at 7.00? After dinner we can watch the match on TV!
>
> See you on Thursday (I hope!).
>
> Lucy

b Now read Kate's answer. Circle the correct phrase.

> **From:** Kate <ksavage@topmail.net>
> **To:** Lucy Lewis <LL1991@netlink.com>
> **Subject:** Re: Dinner
>
> Dear Lucy,
>
> *I'd love to come / I'm sorry, but I can't come* on Thursday. I have an exam on Friday morning and I need to study on Thursday night.
>
> *See you on Thursday. / Maybe see you at the weekend?*
>
> Love,
>
> Kate

c Read the information box about emails.

> 🔍 **Emails**
> **Greetings** *Hi* + name,   *Dear* + name,
> **Closings** *Best wishes*   *Love,* (only family and good friends)
>   *See you* (*on Thursday, soon,* etc.)

d Work in pairs. Write an email to your partner on a piece of paper. Invite him / her to do something, e.g. have dinner, come to a party, see a film, etc. Remember to say when and what time.

e Now exchange emails with your partner. Answer your partner's invitation.

f Give the email to your partner. Read your partner's answer to your email.

⬅ **p.59**

5 A BLOG POST

a Read Eddie's blog. Number the sentences in the correct order 1–7.

> **A BIG DAY**
> by Eddie   *17 hours ago*
>
> [ ] Yesterday was a big day for me. It was the first day of my new job.
>
> [ ] After that, I went to my new office. I got a taxi, because I didn't want to be late.
>
> [ ] I went to bed early, at 9.30. I was really tired, but it was a good day!
>
> [1] I got up at 6.30. I usually get up at 8.00 or 8.30, but yesterday I was very excited!
>
> [ ] I didn't go out for lunch – I had a sandwich in the office. My colleagues usually do that, so I did too.
>
> [ ] I went home at 5.30. I had a pizza for dinner with my girlfriend. After dinner, we watched TV.
>
> [ ] Then I had a shower and had breakfast. I didn't eat very much, because I was a bit nervous.
>
> [ ] When I arrived, the boss introduced me to the other people in the office. Everybody was very friendly.

b Read the information box.

> 🔍 **Showing the order of events**
> ***Then***
> Then I had a shower.
> ***After that***
> After that, I went to my new office.
> ***After* (+ *lunch, dinner,* etc.)**
> After dinner, we watched TV.

c What did <u>you</u> do yesterday? Write a blog about your day. Use *then, after that,* and *after breakfast / lunch,* etc. to put the events in order.

⬅ **p.69**

Listening

🔊 **1.42**

Hello. I'm Rob. I'm from London. I'm a journalist. Today I'm in Poland. I'm not on holiday. I'm here for work.

🔊 **1.45**

Hi. I'm Jenny Zielinski. I'm from New York. Tomorrow's my birthday, and my favourite restaurant in New York is Locanda Verde. It's Italian.

🔊 **1.46**

Waiter Locanda Verde. Good morning. How can I help you?

Jenny Hello. A table for tomorrow, please.

Waiter Tomorrow…er, Tuesday?

Jenny Yes, that's right.

Waiter How many people?

Jenny Three.

Waiter What time?

Jenny Seven o'clock.

Waiter What's your name, please?

Jenny Jenny Zielinski. That's Z-I-E-L-I-N-S-K-I.

Waiter Thank you, Ms, er, Zielinski. OK. So, a table for three on Tuesday at seven.

Jenny Great. Thanks. Bye.

Waiter Goodbye, see you tomorrow.

🔊 **2.26**

1 **A** Great. OK, see you on Tuesday.
  B Yes. Oh, what's your phone number?
  A It's, er, 020 7946 0415.
2 **A** Thank you. What's your address, please?
  B It's 57 King Street. Very near here.
3 **A** Come in, sit down. You're Martin Blunt, right?
  B Yes.
  A And how old are you, Mr Blunt?
  B I'm 39…
4 **A** Thank you very much. Er, one more thing. What's your email?
  B It's james85@ukmail.com.

🔊 **3.2**

What are the top things people look for every day? At number 8, it's…wallets and purses.

At number 7, umbrellas.

At number 6, bank cards – credit cards or debit cards.

At number 5, phone chargers.

And now for the top four.

At number 4, glasses and sunglasses.

At number 3, pens and pencils.

And at number 2, mobile phones.

And at number 1, – yes, that's right – keys. House keys and car keys.

So, try to find a safe place…

🔊 **3.8**

1 Please take out your laptops… All laptops out of cases, please.
2 Please switch off all mobile phones and electronic devices.
3 **A** Excuse me, is this your bag?
  B Oh yes! Thanks very much!
4 **A** Hi. My name's Sam Smith. I have a reservation.
  B Can I see your passport, please?
  A Sure, here you are.
5 **A** OK, Ms Jones. You're in room 315. Here's your key.
  B Thank you very much. Er, where's the lift?

🔊 **3.13**

Man Excuse me, Miss. Is this your phone?

Woman Oh! Yes, it is. Thank you very much.

Man You're welcome. It's a very nice phone! The new iPhone.

Woman Sorry? Oh yes.

Man A souvenir for your family? A football shirt is only £25!

Woman OK. An Arsenal football shirt, please.

Man And a T-shirt?

Woman Yes, and a T-shirt!

🔊 **3.20**

1 **Man** *The New York Times*, please.
  Woman Here you are.
  Man How much is it?
  Woman It's two dollars fifty.
2 **Man** An umbrella, please.
  Woman For how much?
  Man Fifteen euros, please.
  Woman Here you are.
  Man Thanks.
3 **Man 1** A memory card, please.
  Man 2 Two gigs or four?
  Man 1 Two, please. How much is it?
  Man 2 Nine dollars forty-nine.
  Man 1 Is a credit card OK?
  Man 2 Sure.
4 **Woman** A one-way ticket to Oxford, please.
  Man Thirty pounds twenty p, please.
  Woman Here you are.
  Man Thank you.

🔊 **3.25**

Assistant Hi. How can I help you?

Jenny Hi. How much is this tuna salad?

Assistant It's seven twenty.

Jenny OK, fine. And this mineral water, please.

Assistant That's nine dollars seventy cents.

Jenny Here you are.

Assistant Thank you. Have a nice day.

Amy Jenny!

Jenny Amy! Hi, how are you?

Amy I'm fine. How are you?

Jenny I'm fine, too.

Amy What's that?

Jenny Oh, just a salad and some water.

Amy You are good! Look, wait for me. We can have lunch together in the park.

Jenny Sure! Great idea.

Amy Can I have a cheese sandwich, a cappuccino, and a brownie, please?

�))) 4.11

Marina What a lovely card!

Jane Yes, it's from my family.

M Can I see?

J Sure.

M Who's Paul? Is he your brother?

J Yes, he's my brother and Hayley's his girlfriend.

M How old is Paul?

J He's twenty-nine. No, he's thirty.

M What about Susan? Is she your sister?

J No, Susan's my brother Jerry's wife. And Sally's their daughter.

M Oh yes, I remember. The baby in the photo on your phone.

J Yes. She's so beautiful.

M So who's Nicole?

J She's my sister.

M Is John her husband?

J No, he's her boyfriend – they aren't married. Perhaps one day.

M And how old's Nicole?

J She's twenty-six.

M And who's Max?

J He's my dog!

M Ah. What kind of dog is he?

�))) 4.13

1 It's a Jaguar. It's English.

2 It's a Chevrolet. It's American.

3 It's a Mercedes. It's German.

4 It's a Peugeot. It's French.

5 It's a Ferrari. It's Italian.

6 It's a Honda. It's Japanese.

�))) 5.6

Anna My favourite meal of the day is dinner. I usually have dinner at home, but sometimes at a restaurant. I usually have meat or fish and vegetables, and if I'm at a restaurant, I have a glass of wine.

�))) 5.7

Will My favourite meal of the day is lunch. I'm always hungry then. I have lunch at work – we have a canteen there. I have different things for lunch but always with chips – I love chips. Sometimes a burger and chips, sometimes fish and chips. I drink water with my lunch but after lunch I have a coffee, an espresso.

Sarah My favourite meal of the day is breakfast. I usually have it at home, but on Wednesday I have my yoga class and I have breakfast at a café near the yoga studio. At home I have fruit and an egg, and coffee or tea. But at the café I have a croissant and hot chocolate.

�))) 5.15

Taxi driver Where to ma'am?

Eve Hello. To the airport, please.

Taxi driver JFK or Newark?

Eve JFK, please.

Eve Oh dear. The traffic is bad this morning.

Taxi driver Yes. It's terrible. Where are you from?

Eve I'm from Manchester but I live in London. Are you from New York?

Taxi driver No, ma'am, I'm from Puerto Rico.

Eve Oh, do you like New York?

Taxi driver It's a great city, but it's very expensive.

Eve London is very expensive, too. Do you have children?

Taxi driver I have two daughters.

Eve Oh really? I have two sons and a daughter. David and Andrew are at university, and Carla's at school…

Taxi driver OK. Here we are.

Eve How much is that?

Taxi driver That's $87.50.

Eve Oh. Here's $100. Keep the change.

Taxi driver Thanks. Have a good flight!

Eve I need to hurry. I'm late!

Announcement This is the final call for flight BA641 to London Heathrow. Would all passengers please proceed to gate B5?

�))) 5.30

Amy Hi. Sorry I'm late. What time's the show?

Jenny Don't worry. It's at eight o'clock.

Amy What time is it now?

Jenny It's OK. It's only twenty to eight.

Amy What a great show!

Jenny Yes, fantastic. I'm hungry. Do you want a pizza?

Amy What time is it?

Jenny Um, quarter to eleven.

Amy It's late and I'm tired.

Jenny Come on. I know a really good Italian restaurant near here.

Amy Oh, OK. Let's go.

�))) 6.12

I Hannah works for the BBC. She has a son, Kit, who's three years old.

I Hannah, what time do you usually get up?

H I get up at 7.00. But I also get up in the night, because Kit usually calls me. I tell him to sleep, but he usually comes into my bed.

I Do you usually feel tired?

H Yes, I always feel tired!

I Do you have a shower or a bath in the morning?

H I turn on the TV for Kit and then I have a bath in five minutes.

I Do you always have breakfast?

H Yes, I need breakfast every day!

I Where do you have it?

H I have it in a café on the way to work.

I What do you have for breakfast?

H I have a coffee and sometimes I have some toast with avocado. It's delicious.

I What time do you go to work?

H The perfect time to leave the house is at 8.00, but we usually leave at twenty past eight.

I Do you usually need to hurry in the morning?

H Yes, always!

I Do you like mornings?

H Yes. I love mornings.

I Why?

H Because I love my job, and I'm happy to go to work!

�))) 7.2

I Do you go out on Friday night?

P Yes, my husband Andrew and I always go out for a drink or for dinner.

I Where do you go?

P We usually go to our local pub, because they have good food there. We sometimes meet friends there, too.

I What time do you get up on Saturday and Sunday?

P On Saturday at 7.30. On Sunday it depends. At about 9.00?

I What do you usually do on a Saturday?

P I work from 9.00 to 4.00. I'm a hairdresser and we're open on Saturdays. Then after work I go to the supermarket and buy food for the week. In the evening we usually stay at home and watch TV. My husband's a big football fan and he always watches *Match of the Day*.

I Where do you usually have lunch on Sunday?

P With my parents, or sometimes Andrew's parents. My dad makes a very good Sunday lunch – he's the cook in the family.

I Are you tired on Sunday evening?

P Yes, because in the afternoon we need to do housework. Cleaning, washing, things like that.

I Do you do the same thing every weekend?

P Yeah – more or less. Except when we're on holiday.

I What's your favourite part of the weekend?

P Friday night, definitely!

 Go online to listen to the audio and see all the Listening scripts

◀ 7.18

1 **A** Excuse me. Can you answer a few questions?
B Sure.
A Do you like the Alien films?
B I like the first one. It's great. I don't know the others.
A OK, thanks.

2 **A** Do you like the Alien films?
B Yes. They're brilliant.
A Do you like Charlize Theron in *Alien: Prometheus*?
B She's OK, but I prefer Sigourney Weaver.

3 **A** Do you like the Alien films?
B No, I hate science fiction films. I think they're awful.

4 **A** Do you like the Alien films?
B Yes, I love them. And the actors are fantastic.
A Do you like Michael Fassbender?
B I really like him. I think he's great.

5 **A** Do you like the Alien films?
B Sorry, I don't know them.

◀ 7.28

Rob Dad!
Henry Rob, hi!
Rob Hi. This is for you.
Henry For me? It's my favourite wine. Thanks Rob! But why?
Rob For your birthday of course! Happy birthday!
Henry Rob, it isn't my birthday today! My birthday's on the 2nd of July. Today's the 2nd of June.
Rob Oh no!
Henry Don't worry. Come in! Have a glass of wine…

◀ 7.30

Jenny Hello?
Rob Hello. Is that, uh, Jennifer Zielinski?
Jenny Yes. Who's that?
Rob This is Rob Walker.
Jenny I'm sorry, who?
Rob Rob Walker. I work for *London 24seven*. We need to talk about your trip to London in March. Er, you arrive on the 12th of March and you leave on the 19th, is that right?
Jenny I'm really sorry Mr. Walker…er, Rob, but I'm not at work. Today is a holiday here.
Rob A holiday?
Jenny Yes, you know, it's Thanksgiving. I'm at my parent's house, with my family.
Rob Thanksgiving. Of course. Sorry. We don't have Thanksgiving in England.
Jenny No problem. Listen, call me on Monday at work. No, not Monday, Tuesday.
Rob Tuesday the third of December?
Jenny Yes.
Jenny's mom Jenny! Hurry up!
Jenny Talk to you on Tuesday. Thanks for calling.
Rob Bye.
Jenny Bye.

◀ 8.10

1 **A** Excuse me, can I sit here?
B Er, yes, I think it's free.
A Thanks.

2 **A** Can I help you?
B Do you have this T-shirt in large?
A Just a moment. Sorry, we only have small and medium at the moment. I can phone and see if they have a large in another store?
B No, that's OK, thanks.

3 **A** Are you ready to order?
B Yes, can I have the burger, but with salad, not chips?
A Yes, madam, that's fine. And for you, sir?
B The pasta, please.
A And to drink?

4 **A** Hey! You can't sing here.
B Why not?
A Because you need a permit.
B Where can I get a permit?
A You need to go online and look for…

◀ 9.6

1 **W** Oh look! An Inter Milan football shirt. It's perfect for Johnny!
M Yes, good idea. Oh…it's very expensive.
W Football shirts are always expensive. OK. What we can get for Jessica?
M She likes football, too.
W Yes, but she never wears football shirts. What about this bag?
M I don't know. Does she like bags?
W She loves bags…

2 **W** Tom, do we need swimming things?
M I can look at their website. Can you see my camera?
W Yes, here it is. Do you want me to put the camera in the suitcase or in your bag?
M In the suitcase, please. OK, here's the page. Yes, it has a swimming pool.
W Great.

3 **W** Good morning. How can I help you?
M I need a car for three days.
W What kind of car are you looking for?
M A small car. It's just for me.
W Automatic or manual?
M Manual, please.
W Can I see your driving licence?
M Yes, here you are.

4 **M** Is that a number 13?
W Yes. I think it is. No, it's a 23.
M Another 23? I don't believe it! That's the third one. And no 13.
W Another one's coming now. Let's see. Yes. That's a 13.
M At last!

◀ 9.17

Interviewer Hi, Sandra. Tell us a bit about your experience. Where are you working?
Sandra I'm working in a clothes shop called FatFace.
Interviewer What kind of clothes does FatFace have?
Sandra Er, well, clothes for men and women, informal clothes, trousers, T-shirts, sweaters, things like that.
Interviewer What do you do every day?
Sandra Well, er, I help the customers to find the clothes that they're looking for. It's a big shop and it has a lot of things. People sometimes can't see the things that they want.
Interviewer Do you like working there?
Sandra Yes, I love it. The people are really nice to me. I'm making a lot of new friends.
Interviewer Is there anything you don't like?
Sandra Well, we can't sit down, we're standing up all the time. So that's quite hard.

Interviewer But, in general, you're happy?

Sandra Oh, yes. And when my two weeks finish they say I can work here on Saturdays! That's great for me. I really like working in a clothes shop.

Interviewer What do you wear at work?

Sandra We wear clothes from the shop.

Interviewer Are the clothes that you're wearing today from FatFace?

Sandra Yes, they are!

9.21

Steve Hi, Jenny. What a surprise!

Jenny Hi, Steve!

Steve How are you? You're looking great.

Jenny Thanks. I'm well. How about you?

Steve I'm OK. Hey, it's starting to rain. Would you like a coffee?

Jenny Oh, thanks, Steve, but I have a meeting in an hour.

Steve Oh, come on Jenny. I'd like to talk to you.

Jenny OK. A quick coffee.

Steve Jenny, I'd like to ask you something.

Jenny Yes?

Steve There's an exhibition of Picasso at the MoMA next week. I know you love Picasso. Would you like to come with me?

Jenny Listen, Steve. I'm really busy at work at the moment. Next week isn't a good week for me.

Steve Sure. No problem. Maybe we can meet one evening, when you have more time and…have dinner or see a show?

Jenny Listen, Steve. I don't think it's a good idea. But thanks. Oh, look at the time! I need to go. Let's ask for the check.

10.5

Eric Louisa, time to get up.

Louisa OK. What time is it?

Eric It's half past seven. Breakfast is at eight.

Louisa Is it a nice day?

Eric Let's see. Louisa, quick! Come here! Look at that!

Louisa What is it?

Eric Look! Over there.

Louisa Where?

Eric There. In the loch. There! Can't you see? There's something in the loch. It's moving. Can you see it now?

Louisa Yes. What is it?

Eric I don't know. Quick, take a photo with your phone.

Louisa I can't see it now. Can you?

Eric No, I can't. I can't see anything now. Let's see those photos, Louisa. Wow! I don't believe it. Look at that…

10.14

D Are you Kevin Smith?

K Yes, I am.

D What do you do, Kevin?

K I'm a taxi driver.

D And where do you live?

K At 14 Market Street.

D Do you know the suspect, Jason Brown?

K Yes, I know him. He's my friend. We were at school together.

D Where were you yesterday afternoon at 5 o'clock?

K Yesterday at 5 o'clock… I was in my taxi. I was in my taxi all afternoon.

D And at 7 o'clock? Where were you then?

K I was in a pub. The Black Horse.

D Where is it exactly?

K In South Street. Near the station.

D Were you alone?

K No, I was with Jason.

D Were you only with Jason?

K Er, no. My wife was there. And Jason's wife.

D Jason's wife? She was with you?

K Er, yes.

D Are you sure?

K Yes…no…I can't remember.

D You can't remember who you were with yesterday? Very interesting…

11.7

Miriam really liked her job – it was very interesting. I worked from home, so I was with the children a lot and I loved it. In general life was good. It was quite cheap – cheaper than in the UK. We joined a sports club, where the children learned to swim, and I played a lot of tennis, one of my favourite sports.

The people in Durham were very friendly. They often invited us to their homes. It was easy to meet people at the sports club, or at the university where Miriam worked. And there were so many new places to see! At weekends, we visited some of the beautiful national parks. They were very different from English parks! In one park there was a sign saying 'don't disturb the snakes' – Sacha loved it!

I also remember a trip to a country music festival at a blueberry farm. It was fantastic. First we listened to the music, and then we picked a lot of blueberries – they're Elena's favourite fruit. But after that trip she didn't want to eat a blueberry for at least two weeks!

We stayed in Durham for a year. After that we returned to England, because my wife's job finished. But we loved our life in the USA, and we're thinking of going back there in maybe two or three years.

11.22

Rob Oh ****. I don't believe it. Excuse me, this cash machine isn't working. Is there another one near here?

Man Yeah, there's one in HSBC. Go straight on, turn right. Go straight on for a bit and it's on the left.

Rob Thanks.

11.23

Jenny Hello?

Rob Hi, Jennifer?

Jenny Yes.

Rob This is Rob Walker from London 24/7. I'm phoning to check you got the email I sent you.

Jenny Er, what was it about?

Rob It was the information about your hotel for next week.

Jenny Just a second. Yes, here it is. Hotel Indigo, London Street. Where is it exactly?

Rob It's very near Paddington Station. You can get the Heathrow Express train from the airport to the station. It only takes about 15 minutes.

Jenny OK, that's great. Can I walk to the hotel from the station?

Rob Yes, it's very near. Can you see it on the map?

Jenny Ah yes, I have it now.

Rob Turn left when you leave the station. Then go straight on for a bit and turn right into London Street. The hotel's opposite Norfolk Square.

Jenny Great.

Rob I can come to the hotel in the morning on your first day. We can walk to the office together.

Jenny OK. See you then.

Rob Bye.

Jenny Bye.

1A verb *be* (singular): *I* and *you*

🔊 **1.4** Listen and repeat the examples. Then read the rules.

	Full form	Contraction
⊕	I am Helen.	I'm Helen.
	You are Tom.	You're Tom.
⊟	I am not Ellen.	I'm not Ellen.
	You are not Dom.	You aren't Dom.

- *I'm Helen.* **NOT** *i'm Helen.*
- *I'm Helen.* **NOT** *Am Helen.*

🔍 **Negative contractions**
I am not = I'm not
You are not = You aren't **OR** You're not

🔊 **1.5** Listen and repeat the examples. Then read the rules.

❓	⊕	⊟
Am I in class 2?	Yes, **you are.**	No, **you aren't.**
Are you Mike?	Yes, **I am.**	No, **I'm not.**

🔍 **Word order in questions**
| ⊕ | *I'm* in class 2. | *You're* Tom. |
| ❓ | *Am I* in class 2? | *Are you* Tom? |

1B verb *be* (singular): *he, she, it*

🔊 **1.22** Listen and repeat the examples. Then read the rules.

	Full form	Contraction
⊕	I am from the USA.	I'm from the USA.
	You are from Germany.	You're from Germany.
	He is from Italy.	**He's** from Italy.
	She is from Spain.	**She's** from Spain.
	It is from China.	**It's** from China.

- he = man   she = woman   it = thing

🔊 **1.23** Listen and repeat the examples. Then read the rules.

	Full form	Contraction
⊕	I am not from England.	I'm not from England.
	You are not from Poland.	You aren't from Poland.
	He is not from Egypt.	**He isn't** from Egypt.
	She is not from Brazil.	**She isn't** from Brazil.
	It is not from Japan.	**It isn't** from Japan.

🔍 **Negative contractions**
He is not = He isn't **OR** He's not

🔊 **1.24** Listen and repeat the examples. Then read the rules.

❓	⊕	⊟
Am I in class 2?	Yes, you are.	No, you aren't.
Are you from Russia?	Yes, I am.	No, I'm not.
Is he from France?	Yes, **he is.**	No, **he isn't.**
Is she from Turkey?	Yes, **she is.**	No, **she isn't.**
Is it good?	Yes, **it is.**	No, **it isn't.**

🔍 **Word order in questions**
⊕	*She's* from Russia.
❓	*Is she* from Russia?
❓	With *What* and *Where*:
	What's your name? Where are you from?
	Where's he from?

1A

a Complete with *I'm* or *You're*.

Hello. *I'm* Maria. What's your name?

1 Hi. _____ Tony.

2 Hello. _____ your teacher. _____ in my class.

3 _____ in class 4.

4 _____ in room 3.

b Complete with *I'm not* or *You aren't*.

I'm not Tom. I'm Tony.

1 _____ in class 5. You're in class 4.

2 _____ in room 6. You're in room 7.

3 _____ Marina. I'm Marisa.

c Make questions.

You're Sam.   *Are you Sam*?

1 I'm in room 4.   _____?

2 You're Silvia.   _____?

3 I'm in class 3.   _____?

d Complete the conversations. Use contractions where possible.

A Hello. *Are* you Liz?   **B** No, I'*m* not. I'm Maria.

1 **A** _____ I in room 8?   **B** No, you _____. You're in room 6.

2 **A** _____ you in class 4?   **B** No, I _____. I'm in class 5.

3 **A** _____ you Henry?   **B** Yes, I _____. Nice to meet you!

4 **A** _____ I in your class?   **B** Yes, you _____. I _____ your teacher.

 p.6

1B

a Complete with *He's*, *She's*, or *It's*.

A Where's London?

B *It's* in England.

1 **A** Where's Lisa from?
   B _____ from Germany.

2 **A** Where's Ankara?
   B _____ in Turkey.

3 **A** Where's Mario from?
   B _____ from Brazil.

4 **A** Where's St Petersburg?
   B _____ in Russia.

5 **A** Where's Charles from?
   B _____ from England.

6 **A** Where's Anne from?
   B _____ from Switzerland.

7 **A** Where's Benidorm?
   B _____ in Spain.

8 **A** Where's Carlos from?
   B _____ from Mexico.

b Complete with *is*, *'s*, or *isn't*.

A *Is* Ana from Mexico?   **B** No, she *isn't*. She *'s* from Spain.

1 **A** Where _____ Osaka? _____ it in Japan?
   B Yes, it _____.

2 **A** _____ Mark from the USA?
   B No, he _____ from England.

3 **A** Where _____ she from?   **B** She _____ from Rio.

4 **A** _____ Ivan from Poland?
   B No, he _____. He _____ from Russia.

5 **A** _____ Strasbourg in Germany?
   B No, it _____. It _____ in France.

c Complete the conversations with the correct form of *be*. Use contractions where possible.

A *Are* you from Turkey?   **B** No, I'*m not*. I '*m* from Egypt.

1 **A** Where _____ Bergamo? _____ it in Italy?
   B Yes, it _____.

2 **A** Where _____ Alex from? _____ he from Mexico?
   B No, he _____. He _____ from the USA.

3 **A** Where _____ you from?
   B I _____ from Cambridge.

4 **A** What _____ your name?
   B My name _____ Ana. I _____ from Chicago.
   A You _____ from Chicago! I _____ from Chicago, too! It _____ a great city.

p.8

Go online to review the grammar for each lesson

2A verb *be* (plural): *we, you, they*

🔊 **2.6** Listen and repeat the examples. Then read the rules.

	Full form	Contraction
be +	I am English.	I'm English.
	You are Swiss.	You're Swiss.
	He is Spanish.	He's Spanish.
	She is Turkish.	She's Turkish.
	It is Japanese.	It's Japanese.
	We are American.	We're American.
	You are Egyptian.	You're Egyptian.
	They are German.	They're German.

- *you* = singular and plural

- *they* = men, women, and things

🔊 **2.7** Listen and repeat the examples. Then read the rules.

	Full form	Contraction
be −	I am not English.	I'm not English.
	You are not Swiss.	You aren't Swiss.
	He is not Spanish.	He isn't Spanish.
	She is not Turkish.	She isn't Turkish.
	It is not Japanese.	It isn't Japanese.
	We are not American.	We aren't American.
	You are not Egyptian.	You aren't Egyptian.
	They are not German.	They aren't German.

🔍 **Negative contractions**
We are not = We aren't **OR** *We're not*
You are not = You aren't **OR** *You're not*
They are not = They aren't **OR** *They're not*

🔊 **2.8** Listen and repeat the examples. Then read the rules.

be plural, ? and short answers

?	+	−
Am I in room 2?	Yes, you are.	No, you aren't.
Are you Linda?	Yes, I am.	No, I'm not.
Is he Brazilian?	Yes, he is.	No, he isn't.
Is she from Italy?	Yes, she is.	No, she isn't.
Is it good?	Yes, it is.	No, it isn't.
Are we late?	Yes, you are.	No, you aren't.
Are you from Russia?	Yes, we are.	No, we aren't.
Are they Mexican?	Yes, they are.	No, they aren't.

🔍 **Word order in questions**
+ *They're from Russia.*
? *Are they from Russia?*

2B *Wh-* and *How* questions with *be*

🔊 **2.18** Listen and repeat the examples. Then read the rules.

Question word(s)	Verb	Subject	
Who	's	Tom?	He's a friend.
What	's	your email?	johng@gmail.com.
Where	are	you from?	I'm from Brighton in England.
When	's	the concert?	It's on Tuesday.
How	are	you?	I'm fine, thanks.
How old	is	she?	She's ten.

🔍 **Word order**
+ Subject, verb — *They're American.*
? Verb, subject — *Are they American?*
? Question, verb, subject — *Where are they from?*

Contractions with question words
We can contract *is* after question words.
What's her name? = What is her name?
Where's he from? = Where is he from?
How's Anna? = How is Anna?
How old's Jan? = How old is Jan?
Don't contract *is* in a question when the last word is a pronoun (*he, she, it,* etc.).
How old is she? **NOT** ~~How old's she?~~
Where is he? **NOT** ~~Where's he?~~

2A

a Change the **bold** word(s) to a pronoun: *you, he, she, it, we, they.*

Anna and Tom are from London.   *They*'re from London.
1 **Diana and I** are in room 4.   _____'re in room 4.
2 **The Taj Mahal** is in India.   _____'s in India.
3 Are **Mark and James** in Italy?   Are _____ in Italy?
4 Where is **Rosa** from?   Where's _____ from?
5 **Mira and Rita** are Brazilian.   _____'re Brazilian.
6 **Paul** isn't in the hotel.   _____ isn't in the hotel.
7 **You and Sara** are in class 2.   _____'re in class 2.
8 **Jim and I** are from Oxford.   _____'re from Oxford.
9 **Honda and Toyota** are Japanese.   _____'re Japanese.

b Make ⊞ or ⊟ sentences, or ⸮. Use *we, you,* or *they.*

Luisa and I / Brazilian   ⊞ *We're Brazilian.*
You and Henry / teachers   ⊟ *You aren't teachers.*
/ Liz and Tom / in Egypt   ⸮ *Are they in Egypt?*
1 Ana and I / Mexican   ⊟ _____
2 You, Max, and John / in class 4   ⊞ _____
3 / Mike and Peter / English   ⸮ _____
4 / Linda and I / in class 4   ⸮ _____
5 You and Lucy / in class 4   ⊟ _____
6 Lucy and I / on holiday   ⊞ _____

c Complete the conversations. Use contractions where possible.

They *aren't* French. They *'re* Swiss, from Lausanne.
1 A _____ you from the United States?
　B No, we _____ American. We _____ English.
2 A _____ they Spanish?
　B Yes, they _____. They _____ from Madrid.
3 Nikolai is from Moscow. He _____ from St Petersburg.
4 Sorry, you _____ in room 20, you're in room 22.
5 A _____ Adidas American?
　B No, it _____, it _____ German.
6 A _____ we late?
　B Yes, you _____. It _____ 9.30!
7 I _____ Sara Smith, I'm Sara Simpson.
8 They _____ from New York, they're from Texas.
9 A Where's Laura from?
　B She _____ from Recife.
　A _____ Recife in Brazil?
　B Yes, it _____.

⬅ p.12

2B

a Complete with a question word.

~~How~~   How old   What (x2)   When
Where (x2)   Who (x2)

　A *How* are you?
　B Fine, thanks. And you?
1 A _____'s the concert?
　B On Tuesday at 7.30.
　A _____ is it?
　B In the Festival Hall.
2 A _____'s your name?
　B Jessica.
3 A _____ is she?
　B She's my friend, Julia.
　A _____'s she from?
　B Italy.
4 A _____'s your email?
　B It's jbl098@yoohoo.com.
5 A _____'s that?
　B My brother Adrian.
　A _____ is he?
　B He's 25.

b Order the words to make questions.

are how old you?   *How old are you?*
1 she who is?   _____
2 what phone your number is?   _____
3 is where room 4?   _____
4 married is Marta?   _____
5 your English class is when?   _____
6 your number is phone 4960362?   _____
7 is his email what?   _____
8 Pedro how is old?   _____

c Write questions to complete the conversation.

A *What's your name*?   B Pedro Guzman.
A [1]_____?   B Monterrey.
A [2]_____ Monterrey?   B It's in Mexico.
A [3]_____?   B pguzman@gmail.com.
A Thanks. [4]_____?   B 81 8150 9304.
A [5]_____?   B I'm 19.

⬅ p.14

🔵 **Go online** to review the grammar for each lesson

3A singular and plural nouns; a / an

🔊 **3.3** Listen and repeat the examples. Then read the rules.

Singular nouns; a / an

What is it? It's **a book**.   It's **a key**.

It's **an umbrella**.   It's **an ID card**.

- *What is it?* **NOT** ~~*What's it?*~~
- We use *a / an* + singular noun.
- We use *a* + word beginning with a consonant, e.g. *a bag, a phone*.
- We use *an* + word beginning with a vowel, e.g. *an umbrella*.

🔊 **3.4** Listen and repeat the examples. Then read the rules.

Singular nouns; a / an

 What is it? It's a book.    What are **they**? They're **book**s.

 What is it? It's a key.    What are **they**? They're **key**s.

What is it? It's a watch.    What are **they**? They're **watch**es.

 What is it? It's a dictionary.    What are **they**? They're **dictionar**ies.

Spelling rules

Singular	Plural	
1 a bag a holiday	bags holidays	add *-s*
2 a class	classes /ɪz/	add *-es* (after *ch, sh, s, ss, x*)
3 a country	countries	consonant + ~~y~~ *-ies*

🔍 **the**
Look at **the** board.   Open **the** door.   Close **the** windows.
We use *the* + singular or plural nouns, e.g. *the door, the windows*.

3B this / that / these / those

🔊 **3.14** Listen and repeat the examples. Then read the rules.

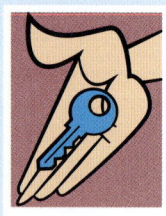 What's **this**? It's a key.    What are **these**? They're keys.

 What's **that**? It's a cat.    What are **those**? They're cats.

- We use *this / these* for things near you (things here).
- We use *that / those* for things that aren't near you (things there or over there).
- *this / that* = singular, *these / those* = plural.
- We also use *this / that / these / those* for people, e.g. *This is my brother. Who are those girls over there?*

🔍 **this, that, these, those**
This, that, these, and *those* are pronouns or adjectives.
This is my book. (= pronoun)
This book is very nice. (= adjective)

here, there, over there

here   there   over there

3A

a Complete the chart.

Singular	Plural
It's a pen.	*They're pens.*
1 _____.	They're phones.
2 It's a watch.	_____.
3 _____.	They're umbrellas.
4 It's a dictionary.	_____.
5 It's a key.	_____.
6 It's a city.	_____.
7 _____.	They're emails.
8 It's a passport.	_____.
9 _____.	They're tablets.

b Write questions and answers.

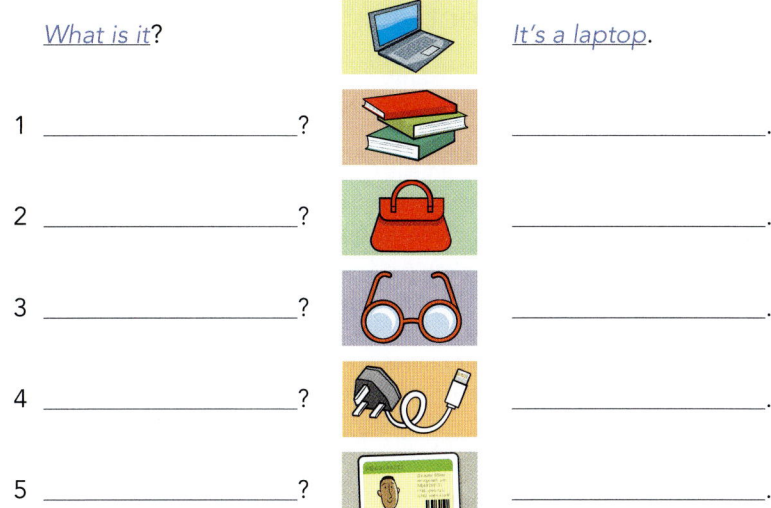

What is it?   *It's a laptop*.

1 _____ ?   _____ .

2 _____ ?   _____ .

3 _____ ?   _____ .

4 _____ ?   _____ .

5 _____ ?   _____ .

p.18

3B

a Look at the pictures. Complete the sentences with *this*, *that*, *these*, or *those*.

This isn't a very good book.

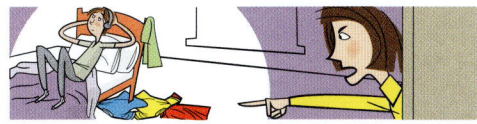

1 Are _____ your T-shirts?

2 _____ are my children.

3 **A** Is _____ your phone over there?
   B No, my phone's here.

4 Look at _____! They're great!

5 Who's _____? Is he your brother?

b Look at the pictures. Circle the correct word(s).

Meg What is (this)/ *that*?
Joe [1] *They're* / *It's* a key ring from New York.
Meg Oh, OK.
Joe And [2] *these* / *those* are sunglasses. [3] *It's* / *They're* great!

Meg Are [4] *these* / *those* mugs?
Joe Yes, [5] *it is* / *they are*. For our coffee. And [6] *that* / *this* is a plate for Jenny.
Meg What [7] *'s that* / *are those*?
Joe [8] *It's* / *They're* a T-shirt. It's for you!
Meg Oh...thanks.

p.21

Go online to review the grammar for each lesson

4

4A possessive adjectives; possessive 's

4.9 Listen and repeat the examples. Then read the rules.

Possessive adjectives	
I'm from Spain.	**My** name is Ana.
You're English.	**Your** name is Ben.
He's from Rome.	**His** name is Marco.
She's Italian.	**Her** name is Clara.
It's a French restaurant.	**Its** name is Chez Marcelle.
We're from Brazil.	**Our** names are Selma and Luis.
You're Polish.	**Your** names are Marek and Ania.
They're from Mexico.	**Their** names are Pedro and Maria.

• *your names, our books, their coats* **NOT** *yours names, ours books, theirs coats*
• *its* = for things or animals, e.g.
  Pizzeria Marco is a good restaurant. **Its** *phone number is 0543387.*
  Senegal is in Africa. **Its** *flag is red, yellow, and green.*
  Look at that fish! **Its** *eyes are yellow.*

> 🔍 **It's or its?**
> *It's = it is* **It's** *a French restaurant.*
> *Its = possessive* **Its** *name is Chez Marcelle.*

4.10 Listen and repeat the examples. Then read the rules.

Possessive 's
This is Jack**'s** car.
Ella is Ben**'s** wife.
Maria is Carlos**'s** sister.
My sister**'s** name is Molly.
This is my parents**'** house.

• We use 's after a person to talk about family and things, e.g. *Ann's brother, Jim's car.*
• We use ' after plural people, e.g. *my brothers' room (= two brothers).*

> 🔍 **'s**
> *She***'s** *American. Her name***'s** *Emma. ('s = is)*
> *Emma is Maria***'s** *daughter. ('s = possessive s)*
>
> **pronunciation of 's**
> *'s usually = /s/, e.g. Jack's or /z/, e.g. Maria's.*
> *'s after a name that ends in s = /ɪz/, e.g. Carlos's = /ˈkɑːlɒsɪz/.*

4B adjectives

4.19 Listen and repeat the examples. Then read the rules.

1 An Audi is **expensive**. It's **fast**.
2 An Audi is an **expensive** car. It's a **fast car**.
3 They're **old houses**. My **glasses** are **new**.
4 He's **tall**. She's **tall**, too.

1 We use adjectives after the verb *be*, e.g.
  An Audi is expensive. **NOT** ~~*An Audi expensive is.*~~
2 We use adjectives before a noun, e.g.
  It's a fast car. **NOT** ~~*It's a car fast.*~~
3 Adjectives are the same for singular and plural:
  It's an old house. They're old houses. **NOT** ~~*They're olds houses.*~~
4 Adjectives are the same for 🧍 and 🧍.

4A

a Complete with *my*, *your* (sing.), *his*, *her*, *its*, *your* (pl.), *our*, or *their*.

I'm American. <u>*My*</u> name is William.

1 They're from France. _____ names are Claire and Françoise.
2 **A** What's _____ name?
   B I'm Julia. Nice to meet you.
3 He's Italian. _____ name is Roberto.
4 It's a good hotel, and _____ restaurant is fantastic.
5 They're Mexican. _____ surname is Romero.
6 I know a very good restaurant in Paris. _____ name is Café des Fleurs.
7 _____ name is Tina. She's Brazilian.
8 Lisa and Amy are American, but _____ husbands are British.
9 **A** We're Jane and Mark Kelley. We have a reservation.
   B You're in room 22. This is _____ key.
10 Here are _____ coffees. The cappuccino is for you, the latte is for Tom, and the Americano is for me.
11 I'm Sally, and this is _____ husband, Tom.
12 **A** Are those your children?
   B No, they aren't. _____ children are over there.

b Write sentences about Sam's family. Use the names and *'s*.

Diana | Peter
Karen | Sam

    Karen / Sam   *Karen is Sam's sister.*
1 Peter / Karen   _____
2 Diana / Sam   _____
3 Karen / Peter   _____
4 Peter / Diana   _____
5 Sam / Peter   _____
6 Diana / Peter   _____
7 Sam / Karen   _____

p.24

4B

a Write sentences with *It's a / an* or *They're* + adjective + noun.

(great)
It's a great restaurant.

1 (old)
_____

2 (black)
_____

3 (new)
_____

4 (big)
_____

5 (expensive)
_____

6 (good)
_____

b Order the words to make sentences.

   blue is bag my   *My bag is blue.*
1 beautiful a day it's
  _____
2 is husband nice very Amy's
  _____
3 questions difficult they're very
  _____
4 phone cheap a is this
  _____
5 photo it's terrible a
  _____
6 Maggie teacher is fantastic a
  _____
7 very is cat old our
  _____
8 restaurant this good a very isn't
  _____
9 long it's a exercise very
  _____
10 is ugly very dog their
  _____
11 expensive Italian bags are very
  _____
12 very this is small room a
  _____

p.27

Go online to review the grammar for each lesson

5A present simple + and −: *I, you, we, they*

🔊 **5.5** Listen and repeat the examples. Then read the rules.

+	−
I **have** cereal for breakfast.	I **don't have** eggs for breakfast. (*don't = do not*)
You **have** rice for lunch.	You **don't have** pasta for lunch.
We **have** coffee for breakfast.	We **don't have** tea for breakfast.
They **have** fish for dinner.	They **don't have** meat for dinner.

- We use the present simple to talk about present habits (= things we usually do), e.g. *I have coffee for breakfast* and things that are always true, e.g. *In my country, we eat a lot of rice.*
- Present simple + and − is the same for *I, you* (singular and plural), *we,* and *they.*
- We make − sentences with *don't,* e.g. *We don't have coffee.* **NOT** ~~We not have coffee.~~

They have fish for dinner.

5B present simple ?: *I, you, we, they*

🔊 **5.12** Listen and repeat the examples. Then read the rules.

?	+	−
Do I need a ticket?	Yes, **you do.**	No, **you don't.**
Do you live near here?	Yes, **I do.**	No, **I don't.**
Do we have good seats?	Yes, **we do.**	No, **we don't.**
Do they like children?	Yes, **they do.**	No, **they don't.**

- Present simple ? is the same for *I, you* (singular and plural), *we,* and *they.*
- We use *do* to make questions: *Do you live here?* **NOT** ~~You live here?~~ **OR** ~~Live you here?~~
- Remember **ASI** to help you with word order in present simple questions: **A** = auxiliary (*do*), **S** = subject (*you, they,* etc.), **I** = infinitive.

Do I need a ticket?

5A

a Write ⊞ or ⊟ sentences.

We (have) *We have sandwiches* for lunch.

I (not like) *I don't like fish*.

1 I (have) _____ for breakfast.

2 We (not drink) _____ in the evening.

3 They (like) _____.

4 You (eat) _____.

5 We (eat) _____ in the evening.

6 I (not have) _____ in my coffee.

7 You (not like) _____.

8 The children (eat) _____.

b Complete with the **bold** verb. Write one ⊞ sentence and one ⊟ sentence.

like
I'm Italian, but I *don't like* pasta.
My friends and I *like* fast food, especially pizzas and burgers.

1 **have**
People in the UK _____ a big lunch – they usually have a sandwich.
We always _____ lunch with my family on Sundays.

2 **eat**
I _____ meat. I'm a vegetarian.
They _____ a lot of fish and rice in Japan.

3 **drink**
You _____ a lot of coffee! It isn't good for you.
They _____ coffee. They only drink tea.

4 **go**
We _____ to restaurants. They're very expensive.
I don't have breakfast at home.
I _____ to a café.   ← p.31

5B

a Complete with *do* or *don't*.

I *don't* live here. I live in the centre.

1 **A** _____ you have children?
   B No, I _____.
2 I _____ like this photo. It's terrible.
3 **A** _____ you want a coffee?
   B No, thanks. I _____ drink coffee.
4 I _____ have brothers and sisters. I'm an only child.
5 **A** _____ you listen to music on the radio?
   B I _____ listen to pop music, but I listen to Classic FM. It's a classical music station.
6 **A** Excuse me, _____ you work here?
   B No, I _____. Sorry.
7 **A** _____ you like American TV series?
   B No, I _____. I _____ watch TV. I read.
8 **A** _____ you have a big family?
   B Yes, I _____. I have two brothers and three sisters.
9 **A** _____ you speak Spanish?
   B No, I _____. I only speak English.
10 **A** _____ you like Saturdays?
   B Yes, I _____. I _____ work at the weekend.

b Order the words to make sentences or questions.

umbrella have do you an? *Do you have an umbrella?*

1 know don't I. _____
2 here you near do live? _____
3 like I football don't. _____
4 sandwich want you a do? _____
5 centre work in the they city. _____
6 sisters two have I. _____
7 French you speak do? _____
8 don't big need a I car. _____
9 German to classes you do go? _____
10 a don't I watch have. _____
11 to in the music car listen you do? _____
12 work I don't Sundays on _____

← p.32

6A present simple: *he, she, it*

🔊6.5 Listen and repeat the examples. Then read the rules.

+	−	?	+	−
I work.	I don't work.	Do I work?	Yes, I do.	No, I don't.
You work.	You don't work.	Do you work?	Yes, I do.	No, I don't.
He works.	He doesn't work.	Does he work?	Yes, he does.	No, he doesn't.
She works.	She doesn't work.	Does she work?	Yes, she does.	No, she doesn't.
It works.	It doesn't work.	Does it work?	Yes, it does.	No, it doesn't.
We work.	We don't work.	Do we work?	Yes, we do.	No, we don't.
You work.	You don't work.	Do you work?	Yes, you do.	No, you don't.
They work.	They don't work.	Do they work?	Yes, they do.	No, they don't.

- Present simple + *he / she / it* = verb + *s*.
- Present simple − *he / she / it* = *doesn't* + verb (*doesn't* = *does not*).
- Present simple ? *he / she / it* = *Does* + *he / she / it* + verb. Remember **ASI** (see **5B** p.100).

Spelling rules 3rd person *s*

I work in an office. I live in Spain.	He works in an office. He lives in Spain.	+ *s*
I watch CNN. I finish work at 8.00.	She watches CNN. The film finishes at 8.00.	+ *es* (after *ch, sh, s, ss, x*)
I study history.	He studies history.	consonant + *y* = *y̶* -*ies*

- Spelling rules for 3rd person *s* are the same as for plural nouns.

🔍 *have, go, do*
These verbs are irregular in the *he / she / it* form of the present simple:
I have   he / she / it **has** /hæz/
I do   he / she / it **does** /dʌz/
I go   he / she / it **goes** /ɡəʊz/

? with *What* and *Where*
What do you do?
Where does he work?

6B adverbs of frequency

🔊6.16 Listen and repeat the examples. Then read the rules.

I **always** have breakfast.
They **usually** finish work at 5.00.
She **sometimes** watches TV in the evening.
He **never** eats meat.
Does she **usually** go shopping on Saturday?
What time do you **usually** get up?

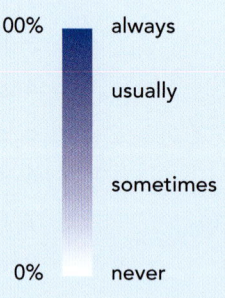

100% — always
usually
sometimes
0% — never

- Be careful with the position of adverbs of frequency:
I always have breakfast. **NOT** ~~Always I have breakfast. I have always breakfast.~~
Does she usually go shopping on Saturday? **NOT** ~~Does usually she go shopping on Saturday? Usually does she go shopping on Saturday?~~
- With *never*, we use a + verb: *He never eats meat.* **NOT** ~~He doesn't never eat meat.~~

He never eats meat.

6A

a Rewrite the sentences.

I live in a flat.   She _lives in a flat_.
1 They read magazines.
   He _____.
2 I study Italian.
   My sister _____.
3 Do you speak English?
   _____ he _____?
4 I don't eat fish.
   My brother _____.
5 Where do you work?
   Where _____ your wife _____?
6 You don't speak Italian.
   Tom _____.
7 Do you like cats?
   _____ she _____?
8 I have two brothers.
   Andrew _____.
9 What do you eat for lunch?
   What _____ he _____?
10 We watch a lot of TV.
   My mother _____.
11 What do you do?
   What _____ your son _____?
12 We don't need a new car.
   Maria _____.

b Put the verb in (brackets) in the correct form.

They _don't live_ near here. (not live)
1 She _____ to the radio in the car. (listen)
2 My brother _____ to university in Manchester. (go)
3 We _____ at the weekend. (not work)
4 _____ Angela _____ with her mother? (live)
5 The programme _____ at 9.30. (finish)
6 She usually _____ fruit for breakfast. (have)
7 We _____ TV at the weekend. (not watch)
8 _____ you _____ tea or coffee? (want)
9 Where _____ your children _____ to school? (go)
10 Linda _____ meat, fish, or eggs. She's a vegan. (not eat)
11 _____ Andrew _____ his new job? (like)
12 Luisa _____ brothers or sisters. (not have)

← p.36

6B

a Order the words to complete the sentences.

drink never coffee I
I never drink coffee after dinner.
1 husband goes my sometimes
   _____ to the gym.
2 have always I
   _____ a shower in the morning.
3 usually we have
   _____ breakfast at home.
4 go I never
   _____ to bed before 12.00.
5 usually go they do
   _____ to work by bus?
6 Jan has sometimes
   _____ a sandwich for lunch.
7 close the does restaurant usually
   _____ late?
8 goes she never
   _____ shopping after work.
9 usually I do
   _____ my homework at the weekend.
10 sometimes make I
   _____ fish for dinner.

b Complete the sentences in the present simple. Use a verb from the list and the adverb in (brackets).

do drink (x2) ~~eat~~ finish get go
have (x3) speak watch

He _never eats_ meat for lunch. (never)
1 Alex _____ _____ to bed very late. (sometimes)
2 We _____ _____ housework at the weekend. (always)
3 Do you _____ _____ lunch at home at the weekend? (usually)
4 I _____ _____ a bath, I _____ _____ a shower. (never, always)
5 My sister _____ _____ up early. (always)
6 I _____ _____ English at work. (never)
7 We _____ _____ TV after dinner. (sometimes)
8 They _____ _____ coffee in the evening. (never)
9 Does your husband _____ _____ work at 7.30 p.m.? (usually)
10 We _____ _____ tea with milk, but I prefer it with lemon. (sometimes)

← p.38

🔄 **Go online** to review the grammar for each lesson

7A word order in questions

🔊 **7.5** Listen and repeat the examples. Then read the rules.

Questions with be

?	Verb	Subject	
	Are	you	tired?
	Are	you	a student?
	Is	this	your coat?
	Is	the shop	near here?
How old	are	you?	
Where	are	you	from?
What time	is	it?	
Why	are	you	late?
Who	are	you?	

- Word order
  - ➕ Subject Verb   *They're American.*
  - ❓ Verb Subject   *Are they American?*

  Where are they from?

🔊 **7.6** Listen and repeat the examples. Then read the rules.

Questions with other verbs

?	Auxiliary	Subject	Infinitive (= verb)
	Do	you	go out on Friday nights?
Where	do	you	go?
What	does	your sister	do?
What music	do	you	like?
When	does	Jane	go to the gym?
How	do	you	spell your name?
Who	does	she	live with?

- Word order = **ASI** (**A**uxiliary **S**ubject **I**nfinitive)
  Do you go out on Friday night?
- **QuASI** (**Qu**estion **A**uxiliary **S**ubject **I**nfinitive)
  Where do you go?

7B imperatives; object pronouns: *me*, *him*, etc.

🔊 **7.12** Listen and repeat the examples. Then read the rules.

Imperatives

➕	Come here! Sit down. Open your books.
➖	Don't talk. Don't worry. Don't be late.

- We use imperatives to give orders or instructions.
- Imperatives are the same for singular and plural.

🔊 **7.13** Listen and repeat the examples. Then read the rule.

Subject pronoun	Object pronoun
I'm your teacher.	Listen to **me**!
You're beautiful.	I love **you**.
He goes to my gym.	I see **him** every week.
She never listens.	Don't talk to **her**.
It's a nice coat!	I want **it** for Christmas.
We aren't friends.	They don't speak to **us**.
They're good books.	I want to read **them**.

- We use object pronouns (*me*, *him*, etc.) as the object of a verb or after prepositions.

7A

a Complete the sentences with a question word from the list.

How (x2)   What (x2)   ~~What time~~
When   Where (x2)   Who

    A _What time_ do you go to bed?
    B At about eleven o'clock.
1 **A** _____ music does she like?
    B Jazz and pop.
2 **A** _____ old is your sister?
    B She's 19.
3 **A** _____ do you want for lunch?
    B A sandwich and a beer, please.
4 **A** _____'s that woman with Bob?
    B His sister.
5 **A** _____ do you have English classes?
    B On Thursdays.
6 **A** _____ do you spell your last name?
    B J-O-H-A-N-S-O-N.
7 **A** _____ does your wife work?
    B In an office.
8 **A** _____ do you usually go on holiday?
    B We usually go to a hot country.

b Order the words to make questions.

    live you do where?   _Where do you live?_
1 your where work do brothers? _____
2 your is this phone? _____
3 film the what start does time? _____
4 Spanish does speak husband your? _____
5 is how family your? _____
6 we late are for class? _____
7 children sushi do your like? _____
8 your finish what does time work wife? _____
9 you are tired why? _____
10 play with you do who tennis? _____

c Complete the questions with *is*, *are*, *do*, or *does*.

    Where _does_ your sister live?
1 _____ football your favourite sport?
2 How _____ you relax at weekends?
3 What films _____ on TV this weekend?
4 _____ you hungry? It's time for lunch.
5 Where _____ you usually have lunch on Sundays?
6 _____ your son play a lot of computer games?
7 How old _____ your teacher?
8 What TV programmes _____ your husband like?
9 _____ you do sport or exercise during the week?

→ p.43

7B

a Complete the sentences with a ⊞ or ⊟ imperative of a verb from the list.

---
close   eat   go   ~~listen~~   make   play
open   read   sit   speak   worry

    Don't listen to Jim. He always says stupid things.
1 It's very cold in here. _____ the window, please.
2 _____ those eggs! I want to make an omelette.
3 _____ the piano! The baby's in bed!
4 _____ slowly, please. I don't understand you.
5 You're very tired. _____ to bed.
6 _____ pasta for lunch! I don't like it.
7 _____ down and _____ your books at page 43.
8 _____ my emails! They're private.
9 _____! It isn't a big problem.

b Complete the sentences with an object pronoun.

    She's a great singer. I really like _her_.
1 I have an old bike, but I don't use _____ very much.
2 Jim likes Sarah, but she doesn't like _____.
3 My children love music. I sing to _____ every night.
4 **A** Is Emma nice?
    B I don't know _____ very well.
5 These are my new shoes. Do you like _____?
6 I'm hungry. Can you make _____ a sandwich, please?
7 Our children usually have lunch with _____ at the weekend.
8 I don't have my car today. Can I go to the concert with _____?

→ p.44

Go online to review the grammar for each lesson

8A can / can't

🔊 8.6 Listen and repeat the examples. Then read the rules.

can / can't: permission and possibility	
+	**−**
I can park here.	**I can't** park there. (*can't = cannot*)
You can sit here.	**You can't** sit there.
He can help us.	**He can't** help us.
We can have lunch outside.	**We can't** have lunch outside.
They can come to dinner tonight.	**They can't** come to dinner tonight.

?	**✓**	**✗**
Can I park here?	Yes, **you can.**	No, **you can't.**
Can he help us?	Yes, **he can.**	No, **he can't.**
Can they come to dinner tonight?	Yes, **they can.**	No, **they can't.**

- We use *can / can't* for permission or possibility.
- *can / can't* is the same for all persons *I, you, he, she,* etc.
- **?** = *Can I sit here?* **NOT** ~~Do I can sit here?~~

> **🔍 Can you drive?**
> We also use *can* to talk about things you know how to do, e.g. *Can you drive? I can't swim. I can play the guitar.*
>
> **you**
> *You* can be personal or impersonal.
> *Can **you** help me?* = personal (singular or plural)
> ***You** can't park on a yellow line.* (= people in general)

8B like / love / hate + verb + -ing

🔊 8.14 Listen and repeat the examples. Then read the rules.

What **do you like doing** at the weekend?
I love cooking.
I like going for a walk.
I don't like studying.
I hate getting up early.

- We use verb + *-ing* after *like, love, hate.*

Spelling rules for *-ing* form		
Infinitive	Verb + *-ing*	Spelling
read fly	I like read**ing**. She doesn't like fly**ing**.	+ *ing*
cycle drive	He loves cycl**ing**. I hate driv**ing** at night.	*e* + *ing*
swim shop	We like swim**ming**. He doesn't like shop**ping**.	one vowel + one consonant = double consonant + *ing*

I hate getting up early.

8A

a Write sentences or questions with *can* or *can't*.

You / play football here
[−] *You can't play football here.*

1 / we sit here
[?] _____

2 I / drink this
[−] _____

3 James / help us tomorrow
[+] _____

4 / you come to lunch on Sunday
[?] _____

5 You / finish work early today
[+] _____

6 We / park here
[−] _____

7 / we watch TV after dinner
[?] _____

8 He / go to school today
[−] _____

b Complete with *can* or *can't* and a verb from the list.

come   drive   go   listen   stay   swim   ~~use~~   walk   watch

You *can't* *use* phones in class.

1 I _____ _____ to work tomorrow. My sister needs the car.

2 **A** _____ I _____ with you?
B No, I'm sorry. We only have one bedroom.

3 **A** _____ we _____ here?
B No, the water's very cold and dirty.

4 The restaurant's very near. We _____ _____ there.

5 Where _____ we _____ for lunch? I'm hungry.

6 You _____ _____ TV when you finish your homework.

7 **A** _____ you _____ to dinner at my house on Saturday?
B I'm sorry, I can't. It's my mother's birthday.

8 **A** Excuse me. You _____ _____ to music in the museum.
B Sorry!

← p.49

8B

a Write the *-ing* form of the verbs.

swim   *swimming*

1 meet   _____
2 stop   _____
3 buy   _____
4 go   _____
5 cry   _____
6 write   _____
7 run   _____
8 cycle   _____
9 get   _____
10 drive   _____
11 sit   _____
12 use   _____
13 put   _____
14 have   _____
15 finish   _____

b Write sentences or questions. Use the correct form of *like* or *love*, and the *-ing* form of the **bold** verb.

I / like / **go** / to bed late
[−] *I don't like going to bed late.*

1 She / like / **cook**
[+] _____

2 you / like / **travel**
[?] _____

3 I / love / **shop** / for presents
[+] _____

4 They / like / **watch** / TV
[−] _____

5 your father / like / **play** / chess
[?] _____

6 George / like / **do** / exercise
[−] _____

7 My mother / love / **read** / detective novels
[+] _____

8 We / like / **fly**
[−] _____

← p.50

Go online to review the grammar for each lesson

9A present continuous

🔊9.2 Listen and repeat the examples. Then read the rules.

Present continuous + and −	
+	**−**
I'm working.	I'm not working.
You're sitting in my chair.	You aren't sitting in my chair.
He's playing football.	He isn't playing football.
She's having a shower.	She isn't having a shower.
It's raining.	It isn't raining.
We're having dinner.	We aren't having dinner.
They're listening to the teacher.	They aren't listening to the teacher.

- We use be + verb + -ing to talk about things that are happening now / at the moment. *I can't talk now. I'm driving.* **NOT** *I drive*.
- See **8B** p.106 for the spelling rules for the -ing form.

Present continuous ?, ✓ and ✗				
Question	**be**	**Subject**	**Verb + -ing**	
	Are	you	working now?	Yes, I am. / No, I'm not.
	Is	she	having a shower?	Yes, she is. / No, she isn't.
	Are	they	listening to the teacher?	Yes, they are. / No, they aren't.
Where	are	you	going?	To a party.
What	's	he	doing?	He's watching TV at home.

🔍 **Word order**

+ Subject, *be*, verb + -ing: **You are working** today.

? *be*, subject, verb + -ing: **Are you working** today?

? Question, *be*, subject, verb + -ing: **Where are you working** today?

9B present continuous or present simple?

🔊9.13 Listen and repeat the examples. Then read the rules.

1 I **work** in an office. I usually **wear** a suit.
2 Today I**'m working** at home. I**'m wearing** jeans.

1 We use the present simple for things we usually do.

   We often use the present simple with *always, usually, sometimes, never*, e.g. *I sometimes have lunch in my office. I never get up early on Saturday.*

2 We use the present continuous for things happening now / at the moment / today.

   Jane's in the kitchen. She's cooking.

   A *What are you doing here?* **B** *I'm waiting for a friend.*

9A

a Write sentences in the present continuous for each picture. Use contractions.

He *'s having* a shower. (have)

1 I can't talk now. I _____. (drive)

2 You _____ the wrong exercise! (do)

3 She _____ at home today. (work)

4 He _____ football. (play)

5 We _____ for an exam. (study)

6 They _____ in the river. (swim)

b Complete the sentences with the verb in (brackets) in the present continuous ⊞, ⊟, or ❓. Use contractions where possible.

She *'s eating* pasta. (eat)

1 **A** Excuse me! You _____ in my seat. (sit)
   B Sorry!
2 **A** Dad _____ this programme. He _____. (not watch, sleep)
   B OK. You can watch your programme then.
3 **A** Hello! What _____ you _____ here? (do)
   B I _____. It's Jim's birthday tomorrow. (shop)
4 **A** I _____ to the gym now. Do you want to come with me? (go)
   B Great idea. I _____ today! (not work)
5 **A** _____ Alice _____ her homework? (do)
   B No, she isn't. She _____ computer games. (play)
6 **A** Do you want my newspaper? I _____ it. (not read)
   B No, thanks. I _____ a film on my laptop. (watch)
7 **A** Is that your brother?
   B No, my brother's over there. He _____ to his friends. (talk)
8 **A** _____ you _____ a good time in Rio? (have)
   B Yes, we are. We _____ a great time! (have)
9 **A** Hello, can I speak to Marisa?
   B Sorry, she _____ her mother on Skype. Who is it? (talk)
   A It's Yuko, from English class. I _____ about tonight's homework. (phone)
10 **A** _____ you _____ up now? You're late for school! (get)
   B Yes, I am. What time is it?

← p.54

9B

a Circle the correct form.

James usually *goes* / *is going* to university in the morning, but today he *studies* / *'s studying* at home.

1 **A** Hi, Sue. Where are you? In the office?
   B No. *I work* / *I'm working* at home today.
2 **A** *Do you do* / *Are you doing* your homework?
   B I don't have any homework today. *I play* / *I'm playing* a video game.
3 My wife is a nurse. *She works* / *She's working* in a children's hospital.
4 We're on holiday in France. *We stay* / *We're staying* in a nice little hotel.
5 **A** Hi. Can you talk or *are you driving* / *do you drive*?
   B *I don't drive* / *I'm not driving*, but I can't talk now. *I have* / *I'm having* lunch with my boss.
6 It always *rains* / *is raining* a lot here in the winter.
7 I usually *have* / *am having* toast for breakfast, but today *I have* / *I'm having* cereal.

b Complete the sentences with the verb in (brackets). Use the present simple or present continuous.

Do you usually *walk* to work? (walk)

1 Oh no! It _____ and I don't have my umbrella. (rain)
2 My father and I _____ dinner together every week. (have)
3 Louise and Carl are on holiday this week. They _____ in Switzerland. (ski)
4 **A** Hi, Sam. _____ you _____ the football match on TV? (watch)
   B No, I _____ my French homework. (do)
5 I always _____ late, and I never _____ time for breakfast. (get up, have)
6 My sister _____ in Thailand at the moment. (travel)
7 **A** What time _____ you usually _____ to bed? (go)
   B At about 11.30.
8 Look. That's my brother over there. Can you see him? He _____ a blue hat. (wear)
9 **A** Hello, Nick. Where _____ you _____? (go)
   B To the gym. I always _____ on Tuesdays. (go)

← p.57

🔵 **Go online** to review the grammar for each lesson

10A *there's a... / there are some...*

🔊 **10.6** Listen and repeat the examples. Then read the rules.

	Singular	Plural
+	**There's** a TV in the room. (*there's = there is*) **There's** a shower.	**There are** two beds in the room. **There are** some pictures.
−	**There isn't** a phone. **There isn't** a bath.	**There aren't** any towels. **There aren't** any books.
?	**Is there** a TV?	**Are there** any pictures?
✓	Yes, **there is**.	Yes, **there are**.
?	**Is there** a bath?	**Are there** any towels?
✗	No, **there isn't**.	No, **there aren't**.

- We use *there is / there are* to say that something or somebody is in a place.
  There's a TV in my hotel room. = *The room has a TV.*

> 🔍 **Word order**
>
> *There's* a swimming pool.
>
> *Is there* a swimming pool?
>
> ***some*** and ***any***
>
> There are **some** towels in the bathroom.
> There aren't **any** towels in the bathroom.
> Are there **any** towels in the bathroom?
>
> - Use *some* with plural nouns in ⊞ sentences. *some* = you don't say exactly how many.
> - Use *any* with plural nouns in ⊟ sentences and ❓.

10B past simple: *be*

🔊 **10.12** Listen and repeat the examples. Then read the rules.

+	−	?	✓	✗
I **was** at home at 8.00.	I **wasn't** at home at 8.00. (*wasn't = was not*)	**Were you** late? **Was she** a singer? **Were they** in Mexico last week?	Yes, **I was**. Yes, **she was**. Yes, **they were**.	No, **I wasn't**. No, **she wasn't**. No, **they weren't**.
You **were** in class yesterday.	You **weren't** in class yesterday. (*weren't = were not*)			
He **was** tired last night.	He **wasn't** tired last night.			
It **was** hot last week.	It **wasn't** hot last week.			
We **were** in London last month.	We **weren't** in London last month.			
You **were** late this morning.	You **weren't** late this morning.			
They **were** famous in the 60s.	They **weren't** famous in the 60s.			

- We use *was / were* to talk about the past.
- Present to past:
  am / is → *was*, *are* → *were*
  He is at home today.
  He was at home yesterday.
- The past of *there is* = *there was*, and the past of *there are* = *there were*.
  There was a party at the school last night.

> 🔍 **Past time expressions**
>
> You can use the past simple with these time expressions:
> **this morning, yesterday, last night, last week, last month, last year**
> *He was late for work this morning.*
> *She wasn't in class last week.*

I was a teacher.

10A

a Complete with the correct form of *there's / there are*, *Is there / Are there*, or *there isn't / there aren't*.

There aren't any pictures on the walls.

1 _____ any free tables in the restaurant?
2 _____ any lifts. Would you like rooms on the ground floor?
3 _____ a bath in the bathroom. It's very big.
4 _____ a gym? I want to do some exercise.
5 _____ a remote control for the TV. Can you ask reception for one?
6 _____ some very ugly pictures in this room.
7 _____ a meeting room in the hotel?
8 _____ some tables in the garden if you want to eat outside.
9 _____ a car park, but we can help you park your car.
10 _____ any clean towels?

b Complete with *a*, *some*, or *any*.

Are there *any* rooms in the hotel?

1 There aren't _____ cars in the car park.
2 There are _____ pillows in the cupboard.
3 There's _____ sauna in the spa.
4 Are there _____ chairs in the garden?
5 Is there _____ TV in the bar?
6 There isn't _____ table in the bedroom.
7 There aren't _____ windows in my room.
8 There are _____ shops in the hotel.
9 There are _____ nice T-shirts in the gift shop.
10 Are there _____ restaurants in the village?

← p.60

10B

a Write sentences or questions with *was* and *were*.

We ⊟
We weren't at home last night.

1 you ?
_____ at school yesterday?
2 James ⊟
_____ very well yesterday.
3 We ⊞
_____ on the plane at 4.00.
4 they ?
_____ in class yesterday?
5 You ⊟
_____ very hungry this morning.
6 I ⊞
_____ in a meeting until 7.00 last night.
7 your sister ?
_____ in London last week?
8 It ⊞
_____ a terrible film.
9 I ⊟
_____ at home last weekend.
10 Sarah and Emma ⊞
_____ tired this morning.

b Complete the conversations with *was*, *wasn't*, *were*, or *weren't*.

1 A Where *were* you last night?
   B I _____ at work all evening.
   A No, you _____. You _____ with Miriam!
   B No, I _____!

2 A _____ Freddie Mercury an actor?
   B No, he _____. He _____ a singer with Queen.

3 A _____ you in Milan yesterday?
   B No, we _____. We _____ in Rome.

4 A _____ the film good?
   B No, it _____. It _____ very slow!

← p.62

Go online to review the grammar for each lesson

11A past simple: regular verbs

11.3 Listen and repeat the examples. Then read the rules.

+	−	?	✓	✗
I arrived at the airport at 7.00.	**I didn't arrive** at the airport at 7.00.	**Did you watch TV** yesterday?	Yes, **I did**.	No, **I didn't**.
You finished the book.	**You didn't finish** the book.	**Did she walk** to work?	Yes, **she did**.	No, **she didn't**.
He wanted a coffee.	**He didn't want** a coffee.	**Did they play** tennis?	Yes, **they did**.	No, **they didn't**.
She liked the film.	**She didn't like** the film.			
It rained yesterday.	**It didn't rain** yesterday.			
We studied Spanish at school.	**We didn't study** Spanish at school.			
They stopped at a café.	**They didn't stop** at a café.			

- We use the past simple to talk about the past.
- The past simple is the same for all persons, e.g. *I arrived, he arrived, they arrived*, etc.
- We use *did* (not *do / does*) to make questions and negatives in the past simple.
- [−] = *I didn't arrive at the airport.* **NOT** ~~*I didn't arrived*~~
- [?] = *Did you watch TV...?* **NOT** ~~*Did you watched*~~

Spelling rules for regular verbs

work finish	work**ed** finish**ed**	verb + *ed*
live change	live**d** change**d**	verb ending in *e* + *d*
cry study	cr**ied** stud**ied**	verbs with final consonant + *y* = ~~*y*~~ + *ied*
stop travel	stop**ped** travel**led**	verbs that end consonant–vowel–consonant double final consonant + *ed*

11B past simple irregular verbs: *get, go, have, do*

11.13 Listen and repeat the examples. Then read the rules.

+	−
I got up late yesterday.	**I didn't get up** late yesterday.
He went to work by car.	**He didn't go** to work by car.
She had eggs for breakfast.	**She didn't have** eggs for breakfast.
We did yoga yesterday.	**We didn't do** yoga yesterday.
They did their homework last night.	**They didn't do** their homework last night.

?	✓	✗
Did you get up late yesterday?	Yes, **I did**.	No, **I didn't**.
Did he go to work by car yesterday?	Yes, **he did**.	No, **he didn't**.
Did they do their homework last night?	Yes, **they did**.	No, **they didn't**.

?	✓
What time did you get up?	At eight o'clock.
Where did you go on Saturday?	We **went** to the beach.
Where did you have lunch?	At school.
What did you do last night?	We **had** dinner with friends.

- *get, go,* and *have*, and *do* are irregular verbs in the past tense.
- **Present to past**

  [+]
  *I **get** up early. → I **got** up early.*
  *I **go** to school. → I **went** to school.*
  *I **have** breakfast. → I **had** breakfast.*
  *I **do** my homework. → I **did** my homework.*

  [−]
  *I **don't get** up early. → I **didn't get** up early.*
  *I **don't go** to school. → I **didn't go** to school.*
  NOT ~~*I didn't got up early.*~~ / ~~*I didn't went to school.*~~ etc.

  [?]
  ***Do** you **have** breakfast? → **Did** you **have** breakfast?*
  ***Do** you **do** your homework? → **Did** you **do** your homework?*
  NOT ~~*Did you had breakfast?*~~ / ~~*Did you did your homework?*~~ etc.

- Remember word order in questions:
  ASI (**A**uxiliary, **S**ubject, **I**nfinitive) *Did you get up early?*
  QuASI (**Qu**estion word, **A**uxiliary, **S**ubject, **I**nfinitive)
  What time did you get up?

did / didn't

We use *did / didn't* to make questions and negatives in the past, e.g.
***Did** you go to class?*
*I **didn't** have breakfast this morning.*
Here, *did / didn't* = an auxiliary verb.
But *did* can also be a normal verb, e.g. *I **did** my homework at the weekend.*

11A

a Write the sentences in the past simple.

He watches a lot of TV.   *He watched a lot of TV.*

1 They work in a bank.   _____

2 He finishes work late.   _____

3 We live in Brazil.   _____

4 I carry a big bag.   _____

5 She walks to work.   _____

6 The train stops in Barcelona.   _____

7 We play tennis.   _____

8 You talk a lot!   _____

9 I relax at the weekend.   _____

10 He waits for the bus.   _____

11 They travel by train.   _____

12 She needs a new coat.   _____

b Complete the conversations with the verb in (brackets) in the past simple ⊞, ⊟, or ⍰.

(play) A *Did* you *play* golf last weekend?
       B Yes, I *played* on Saturday.

1 (park) A Where _____ you _____ the car?
         B I _____ it near the restaurant.

2 (finish) A _____ you _____ your homework?
         B No, I _____ it. It was very difficult.

3 (study) A What _____ you _____ at university?
         B I _____ economics.

4 (like) A _____ you _____ the concert?
         B No, I _____ it very much. The singers were terrible.

5 (watch) A _____ you _____ TV last night?
         B Yes, we _____ a very good programme.

6 (close) A _____ you _____ the door when you went out?
         B Of course I _____ it!

7 (cry) A _____ you _____ at the end of the film?
         B Yes, I _____ a lot!

8 (arrive) A What time _____ you _____ in Tokyo?
         B We _____ very late, about 1.00 a.m.

⬅ p.66

11B

a Change from present to past. Use the time expression in (brackets).

I don't go the gym.

I didn't go to the gym yesterday.

1 I have eggs for breakfast.
   _____ this morning.

2 Does she go to Spanish classes?
   _____ last year?

3 We don't have lunch at home.
   _____ last week.

4 Mike doesn't go to work by car.
   _____ yesterday.

5 They go to school by bus.
   _____ yesterday.

6 What time do you get up?
   _____ this morning?

7 Do you do sport or exercise?
   _____ last weekend?

8 You don't do the housework.
   _____ yesterday.

9 I don't get up early.
   _____ this morning.

b Complete with the verb in (brackets) in the past simple ⊞, ⊟, or ⍰.

(go) A *Did* you *go* to bed early last night?
     B Yes, I did. I *went* to bed at 9.30!

1 (have) A What _____ you _____ for lunch today?
         B I _____ fish.

2 (do) A _____ you _____ the housework?
        B No, but I _____ my English homework.

3 (go) A Where _____ you _____ last night?
        B I _____ _____ out. I stayed at home.

4 (get up) A What time _____ the children _____?
          B They _____ very late. They were tired.

5 (have) A What _____ you _____ for breakfast?
         B I _____ _____ breakfast. I wasn't hungry. I just _____ a coffee.

6 (go) A _____ Pedro _____ to judo last week?
        B He _____ on Monday, but he _____ _____ on Wednesday because he wasn't very well.

⬅ p.68

🔵 **Go online** to review the grammar for each lesson

12A past simple: regular and irregular verbs

🔊 **12.6** Listen and repeat the examples. Then read the rules.

be	
I **was** at home last night	I **wasn't** at home last night.
You **were** very late.	You **weren't** very late.
He **was** a teacher.	He **wasn't** a teacher.
She **was** in bed at 10.00.	She **wasn't** in bed at 10.00.
It **was** cold yesterday.	It **wasn't** cold yesterday.
You **were** tired last night.	You **weren't** tired last night.
We **were** in Spain in May.	We **weren't** in Spain in May.
They **were** nice rooms.	They **weren't** nice rooms.
Was she tired?	Yes, **she was**.
Were they at school?	No, **they weren't**.
Where **were you** at 8.00 this morning?	**I was** on the bus.

- *was / were* is the past of *am / is / are*.
- To make questions change the order:
  *She **was** at home.*

  ***Was** she at home?*

🔊 **12.7** Listen and repeat the examples. Then read the rules.

Regular verbs	
I **play**ed tennis yesterday.	I **didn't play** tennis yesterday.
They **work**ed all weekend.	They **didn't work** all weekend.
Did you like the film?	Yes, **I did**. No, **I didn't**.
Where **did they stay** in London?	They **stayed** in a hotel in Chelsea.

- For regular verbs add *-ed* or *-d* to the infinitive to make the past simple.

🔊 **12.8** Listen and repeat the examples. Then read the rules.

Irregular verbs	
I **got up** late yesterday.	I **didn't get up** late yesterday.
They **had** lunch at a restaurant.	They **didn't have** lunch at a restaurant.
Did you go on holiday last summer?	Yes, **I did**. No, **I didn't**.
Where **did you go** on holiday?	We **went** to Brazil.

- Some verbs are irregular in the past simple, e.g. *go → went*.
- To make negatives of regular and irregular verbs, we use *didn't* + the infinitive, e.g. *I didn't like the film. They didn't go to class.*
- To make questions with regular and irregular verbs, we use *Did* + person + the infinitive, e.g. *Did you like the film? Did they go to class?*
- Remember word order in questions:
  ASI (**A**uxiliary, **S**ubject, **I**nfinitive) *Did she want to come?*
  QuASI (**Qu**estion word, **A**uxiliary, **S**ubject, **I**nfinitive) *What time did they get up?*
- There is a list of regular and irregular verbs on p.133.

12A

Complete the story with the verbs in (brackets) in the past simple ⊞, ⊟, or ⍰.

Last summer my family and I _went_ (go) to Italy for a holiday. We ¹_____ (rent) a house in Umbria, in central Italy, about 5 km from a village called Gubbio. The weather ²_____ (be) fantastic, hot and sunny during the day, but cold at night. We ³_____ (do) different things every day. Sometimes we ⁴_____ (go) to Perugia or Assisi and ⁵_____ (visit) churches and art galleries. On other days we ⁶_____ (stay) in the house. It ⁷_____ (have) a swimming pool in the garden, so the children ⁸_____ (be) happy. One afternoon an old woman ⁹_____ (arrive) at the door.

'Good afternoon,' she ¹⁰_____ (say). 'I'm your neighbour. Are your children at home?'

'Yes,' I ¹¹_____ (answer). 'I think so. Why?'

'Because about an hour ago I ¹²_____ (see) a small boy near the village. I think he was your son.'

I ¹³_____ (look) out of the window. My daughter ¹⁴_____ (be) in the swimming pool, but my son ¹⁵_____ (not be) there.

'Where ¹⁶_____ you _____ (see) him?' I ¹⁷_____ (ask). '¹⁸_____ you _____ (talk) to him?'

'He was on the road to the village, but I ¹⁹_____ (not speak) to him,' the old woman ²⁰_____ (say).

'Come on,' I ²¹_____ (tell) my husband. 'We need to go to the village.'

The old woman ²²_____ (wait) at the house with my daughter and we ²³_____ (go) to the village.

My son ²⁴_____ (be) outside a café. He ²⁵_____ (have) a big ice cream in his hand.

'Why ²⁶_____ you _____ (leave) the house?' I asked him. 'We ²⁷_____ (be) really worried.'

'I ²⁸_____ (want) an ice cream,' he said.

◀ p.73

Numbers

1 0–10

a 🔊 1.8 Listen and repeat the numbers.

0 <u>ze</u>ro /ˈzɪərəʊ/
(also 'oh' /əʊ/ in phone numbers)
1 one /wʌn/
2 two /tuː/
3 three /θriː/
4 four /fɔː/
5 five /faɪv/
6 six /sɪks/
7 <u>se</u>ven /ˈsevn/
8 eight /eɪt/
9 nine /naɪn/
10 ten /ten/

> 🔍 **Word stress**
> <u>ze</u>ro = **ze**ro   <u>se</u>ven = **se**ven

b Cover the words. Say the numbers.

ACTIVATION Count from 0–10 and from 10–0.

← **p.7**

2 11–100

11–20

a 🔊 2.21 Listen and repeat the numbers.

11 e<u>le</u>ven /ɪˈlevn/
12 twelve /twelv/
13 thir<u>teen</u> /θɜːˈtiːn/
14 four<u>teen</u> /fɔːˈtiːn/
15 fif<u>teen</u> /fɪfˈtiːn/
16 six<u>teen</u> /sɪksˈtiːn/
17 seven<u>teen</u> /ˌsevnˈtiːn/
18 eigh<u>teen</u> /eɪˈtiːn/
19 nine<u>teen</u> /naɪnˈtiːn/
20 <u>twen</u>ty /ˈtwenti/

21–100

b 🔊 2.22 Listen and repeat the numbers.

21 <u>twenty</u>-one /ˌtwenti ˈwʌn/
22 <u>twenty</u>-two /ˌtwenti ˈtuː/
30 <u>thir</u>ty /ˈθɜːti/
33 <u>thir</u>ty-three /ˌθɜːti ˈθriː/
40 <u>for</u>ty /ˈfɔːti/
44 <u>for</u>ty-four /ˌfɔːti ˈfɔː/
50 <u>fif</u>ty /ˈfɪfti/
55 <u>fif</u>ty-five /ˌfɪfti ˈfaɪv/
60 <u>six</u>ty /ˈsɪksti/
66 <u>six</u>ty-six /ˌsɪksti ˈsɪks/
70 <u>se</u>venty /ˈsevnti/
77 <u>se</u>venty-<u>se</u>ven /ˌsevnti ˈsevn/
80 <u>eigh</u>ty /ˈeɪti/
88 <u>eigh</u>ty-eight /ˌeɪti ˈeɪt/
90 <u>nine</u>ty /ˈnaɪnti/
99 <u>nine</u>ty-nine /ˌnaɪnti ˈnaɪn/
100 a <u>hun</u>dred /ə ˈhʌndrəd/

> 🔍 **Word stress – be careful!**
> 30 **thir**ty   13 thir**teen**   40 **for**ty   14 four**teen**, etc.

ACTIVATION Cover the words. Say the numbers.

← **p.15**

Countries and nationalities

1 COUNTRIES

a 🔊 **1.18** Listen and repeat the countries.

1 Brazil /brəˈzɪl/
2 China /ˈtʃaɪnə/
3 Egypt /ˈiːdʒɪpt/
4 England /ˈɪŋglənd/
  the UK* /ˈjuː keɪ/
5 France /frɑːns/
6 Germany /ˈdʒɜːməni/
7 Italy /ˈɪtəli/
8 Japan /dʒəˈpæn/
9 Mexico /ˈmeksɪkəʊ/
10 Poland /ˈpəʊlənd/
11 Russia /ˈrʌʃə/
12 Spain /speɪn/
13 Switzerland /ˈswɪtsələnd/
14 Turkey /ˈtɜːki/
15 the United States (the USA)
  /juːˈnaɪtɪd steɪts/

*the UK = England, Scotland, Wales, and Northern Ireland

> 🔍 **CAPITAL letters**
> Brazil **NOT** ~~brazil~~.

b Write your country: _____. Practise saying it.

ACTIVATION Cover the words. Look at the photos.
Say the countries.
← p.8

2 NATIONALITIES

a 🔊 **2.1** Listen and repeat the countries and nationalities.

	Country	Nationality
🇧🇷	Brazil	Brazilian /brəˈzɪliən/
🇨🇳	China	Chinese /tʃaɪˈniːz/
🇪🇬	Egypt	Egyptian /iˈdʒɪpʃn/
🏴	England	English /ˈɪŋglɪʃ/
🇫🇷	France	French /frentʃ/
🇩🇪	Germany	German /ˈdʒɜːmən/
🇮🇹	Italy	Italian /ɪˈtæliən/
🇯🇵	Japan	Japanese /dʒæpəˈniːz/
🇲🇽	Mexico	Mexican /ˈmeksɪkən/
🇵🇱	Poland	Polish /ˈpəʊlɪʃ/
🇷🇺	Russia	Russian /ˈrʌʃn/
🇪🇸	Spain	Spanish /ˈspænɪʃ/
🇨🇭	Switzerland	Swiss /swɪs/
🇹🇷	Turkey	Turkish /ˈtɜːkɪʃ/
🇺🇸	the United States	American /əˈmerɪkən/
🇬🇧	the UK	British /ˈbrɪtɪʃ/

> 🔍 **Word stress**
> For most countries, the word stress is the same on the country and the nationality, e.g. *Brazil, Brazilian.*
> Sometimes it's different:
> *China → Chinese   Egypt → Egyptian*
> *Italy → Italian   Japan → Japanese*

b Write your nationality: _____. Practise saying it.

c Read about countries and languages. What's the language in your country?

> 🔍 **Countries and languages**
> The word for a language is sometimes the same as the nationality.
> **England:** nationality *English*, language *English*
> Some are different, e.g.
> **Brazil:** nationality *Brazilian*, language *Portuguese*
> **Egypt:** nationality *Egyptian*, language *Arabic*

ACTIVATION Cover the words. Look at the flags.
Say the countries and nationalities.
← p.12

> 🔵 **Go online** to review the vocabulary for each lesson

The classroom

1 THINGS IN THE CLASSROOM

a 🔊 **1.38** Listen and repeat the words.

1 the board /bɔːd/
2 the door /dɔː/
3 a window /ˈwɪndəʊ/
4 a chair /tʃeə/
5 a coat /kəʊt/
6 a table /ˈteɪbl/
7 a laptop /ˈlæptɒp/
8 a dictionary /ˈdɪkʃənri/
9 a piece of paper /piːs əv ˈpeɪpə/
10 a pen /pen/
11 a bag /bæg/

b Cover the words. Look at the picture.
Say the things.

ACTIVATION In pairs, point to things in the
classroom. Your partner says the word.

What is it?) (*It's the board.*
How do you spell it?) (*B-O-A-R-D.*

2 CLASSROOM LANGUAGE

🔊 **1.39** Listen and repeat the phrases.

The teacher says…

1 Look at the board, please.

2 Open your books.

3 Go to page 10.

4 Close your books.

5 Stand up, please.

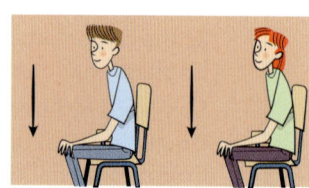

6 Sit down.

You say…

W-i-n-d-o-??

7 How do you spell it?

8 Sorry? Can you repeat that, please?

Thank you.

9 Excuse me. What's *gracias* in English?

???

10 I don't understand.

What's the capital of Australia? ???

11 I don't know.

12 Sorry I'm late.

ACTIVATION Cover the phrases. Look at the pictures. Say the phrases.

🔙 p.10

Small things

a 🔊 **3.1** Listen and repeat the words.

1 a (mobile) phone /fəʊn/
2 a watch /wɒtʃ/
3 a tablet /ˈtæblət/
4 a wallet /ˈwɒlɪt/
   a purse /pɜːs/
5 a pencil /ˈpensl/
6 a notebook /ˈnəʊtbʊk/
7 glasses /ɡlɑːsɪz/
8 a photo /ˈfəʊtəʊ/

9 a (phone) charger /ˈtʃɑːdʒə/
10 an ID card /aɪˈdiː kɑːd/
   a passport /ˈpɑːspɔːt/
11 an umbrella /ʌmˈbrelə/
12 a camera /ˈkæmərə/
13 a credit card /ˈkredɪt kɑːd/
   a debit card /ˈdebɪt kɑːd/
14 a key /kiː/
15 a newspaper /ˈnjuːzpeɪpə/

> 🔍 **a / an**
> **a** bag, **a** key
> **an** ID card, **an** umbrella
>
> **ph**
> ph = /f/, e.g. **ph**one, **ph**oto

b Cover the words. Look at the photo. Say the things.

 p.18

People and family

1 PEOPLE

a 🔊**4.2** Listen and repeat the words.

1 a boy /bɔɪ/
2 a girl /gɜːl/
3 a man /mæn/
4 a woman /ˈwʊmən/
5 children /ˈtʃɪldrən/
6 friends /frendz/

b 🔊**4.3** Listen and repeat the irregular plurals.

🔍 **Irregular plurals**

Singular	Plural
a child	children
a man	men
a woman	women
a person	people

ACTIVATION Look at the photos in **a**. Say the words in singular and plural.

(*a boy   boys*

2 FAMILY

a 🔊**4.4** Listen and repeat the words.

1 husband /ˈhʌzbənd/
2 wife /waɪf/
3 mother /ˈmʌðə/
4 father /ˈfɑːðə/
5 son /sʌn/
6 daughter /ˈdɔːtə/
7 brother /ˈbrʌðə/
8 sister /ˈsɪstə/
9 grandmother /ˈɡrænmʌðə/
10 grandfather /ˈɡrænfɑːðə/
11 boyfriend /ˈbɔɪfrend/
12 girlfriend /ˈɡɜːlfrend/

🔍 **parents**

mother + father = parents /ˈpeərənts/ **NOT** fathers

grandmother + grandfather = grandparents /ˈɡrænpeərənts/

ACTIVATION Cover the words. Look at the photos. Say the family members.

🔵 p.24

Adjectives

1 COLOURS

🔊 **4.16** Listen and repeat the words.

1

black /blæk/

2

blue /bluː/

3

brown /braʊn/

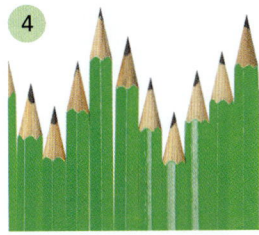
4

green /griːn/

5

grey /greɪ/

6

orange /ˈɒrɪndʒ/

7

pink /pɪŋk/

8

red /red/

9

white /waɪt/

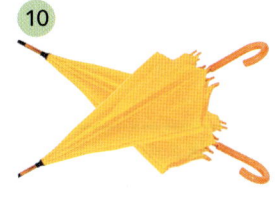
10

yellow /ˈjeləʊ/

ACTIVATION Cover the words. Look at the photos. Ask and answer.

What colour is it? (*It's black.*

What colour are they? (*They're blue.*

2 COMMON ADJECTIVES

a 🔊 **4.17** Listen and repeat the words.

1 **2**

big /bɪg/   small /smɔːl/

3

old /əʊld/

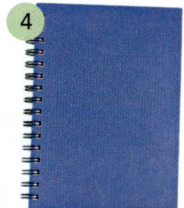
4

new /njuː/

5 **6**

fast /fɑːst/   slow /sləʊ/

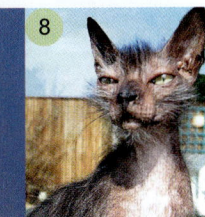
7 **8**

beautiful /ˈbjuːtɪfl/   ugly /ˈʌgli/

9 **10**

cheap /tʃiːp/   expensive /ɪkˈspensɪv/

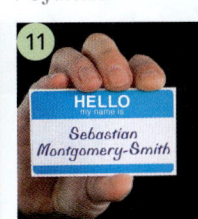
11

long /lɒŋ/

12

short /ʃɔːt/

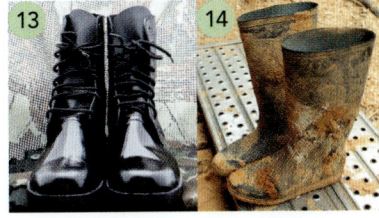
13 **14**

clean /kliːn/   dirty /ˈdɜːti/

15

easy /ˈiːzi/

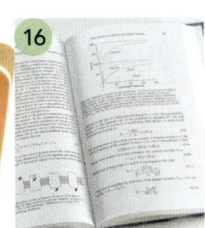
16

difficult /ˈdɪfɪkəlt/

b Cover the words. Look at the photos. Say the adjectives.

ACTIVATION Test a partner.

What's the opposite of new?) (*Old. What's the opposite of _____?*

d 🔊 **4.18** Listen and repeat the positive and negative adjectives.

> 🔍 **Positive and negative adjectives**
> ✓ = good   ✓✓ = very good   ✓✓✓ = great / fantastic
> ✗ = bad   ✗✗ = very bad   ✗✗✗ = awful / terrible
>
> **very**
> You can use **very** before adjectives, e.g. *A Ferrari is **very** expensive. It's a **very** fast car.*

← p.26

Food and drink

a 🔊 **5.2** Listen and repeat the words.

Food

1 fish /fɪʃ/

2 meat /miːt/

3 pasta /ˈpæstə/

4 rice /raɪs/

5 eggs /egz/

6 yogurt /ˈjɒgət/

7 vegetables /ˈvedʒtəblz/

8 potatoes /pəˈteɪtəʊz/

9 salad /ˈsæləd/

10 fruit /fruːt/

11 bread /bred/

12 butter /ˈbʌtə/

13 cheese /tʃiːz/

14 sugar /ˈʃʊgə/

15 a sandwich /ˈsænwɪtʃ/

16 cereal /ˈsɪəriəl/

17 chocolate /ˈtʃɒklət/

Drinks

18 coffee /ˈkɒfi/

19 tea /tiː/

20 milk /mɪlk/

21 water /ˈwɔːtə/

22 orange juice /ˈɒrɪndʒ dʒuːs/

23 wine /waɪn/

24 beer /bɪə/

b 🔊 **5.3** Listen and repeat the words and phrases in the box.

ACTIVATION Cover the words in **a**. Look at the photos.
Say the words.
🔴 **p.30**

🔍 **Meals**
breakfast (in the morning)
lunch (in the afternoon)
dinner (in the evening)

Verbs: have, eat, drink
I **have** breakfast at 8.00.
I **have** cereal and tea.
I **eat** a lot of fruit.
I **drink** tea with milk.

eat

drink

Common verb phrases 1

a 🔊 **5.13** Listen and repeat the phrases.

1 **live** in a flat /lɪv ɪn ə flæt/

2 **have** breakfast (lunch / dinner)
/hæv 'brekfəst/ (lʌntʃ / 'dɪnə)

3 **watch** TV /wɒtʃ tiː'viː/

4 **listen** to the radio
/'lɪsn tə ðə 'reɪdiəʊ/

5 **read** the newspaper
/riːd ðə 'njuːzpeɪpə/

6 **eat** fast food /iːt fɑːst fuːd/

7 **drink** tea /drɪŋk tiː/

Good morning!

8 **speak** English /spiːk 'ɪŋglɪʃ/

9 **want** a coffee /wɒnt ə 'kɒfi/

10 **have** a dog /hæv ə dɒg/

11 **like** cats /laɪk kæts/

12 **work** in a bank /wɜːk ɪn ə bæŋk/

13 **study** Spanish /'stʌdi 'spænɪʃ/

14 **go** to English classes
/gəʊ tə 'ɪŋglɪʃ 'klɑːsɪz/

15 **need** a new car /niːd ə njuː kɑː/

b 🔊 **5.14** Cover the phrases. Listen and say the phrase.

ACTIVATION Ask and answer with a partner in a different order.

Do you drink tea? ⟩ ⟨ *Yes, I do.* ⟨ *No, I don't.*

1 ⟩) *in a flat* ⟨ *live in a flat*

← p.33

Go online to review the vocabulary for each lesson

Jobs and places of work

1 WHAT DO THEY DO?

a 🔊 **6.1** Listen and repeat the words.

1 a <u>tea</u>cher /ˈtiːtʃə/

2 a <u>doc</u>tor /ˈdɒktə/

3 a nurse /nɜːs/

4 a <u>jour</u>nalist /ˈdʒɜːnəlɪst/

5 a <u>wai</u>ter /ˈweɪtə/
a <u>wai</u>tress /ˈweɪtrəs/

6 a shop as<u>sis</u>tant /ˈʃɒp əsɪstənt/

7 a re<u>cep</u>tionist /rɪˈsepʃənɪst/

8 a po<u>lice</u>man /pəˈliːsmən/
a po<u>lice</u>woman /pəˈliːswʊmən/

9 a <u>fac</u>tory <u>wor</u>ker /ˈfæktəri ˈwɜːkə/

10 a <u>ta</u>xi <u>dri</u>ver /ˈtæksi ˈdraɪvə/

b Cover the words. Ask and answer in pairs.

What does he do?) (*He's a teacher.*
What does she do?) (*She's a...*

c 🔊 **6.2** Listen and repeat the sentences.

I work for an A<u>me</u>rican <u>com</u>pany. /ˈkʌmpəni/
I'm at uni<u>ver</u>sity. /juːnɪˈvɜːsəti/
I'm a <u>stu</u>dent. /ˈstjuːdnt/
I study eco<u>no</u>mics. /ekəˈnɒmɪks/
I'm at school.
I'm unem<u>ployed</u> at the <u>mo</u>ment. /ʌnɪmˈplɔɪd/
I'm re<u>ti</u>red. /rɪˈtaɪəd/

d What do <u>you</u> do?
I _____.

2 WHERE DO THEY WORK?

a 🔊 **6.3** Listen and repeat the phrases.

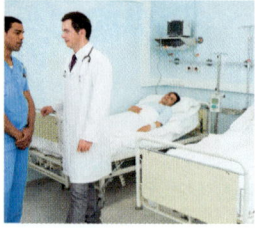

1 in a <u>hos</u>pital /ˈhɒspɪtl/

2 in a shop /ʃɒp/

3 in a <u>res</u>taurant /ˈrestrɒnt/

4 in an <u>o</u>ffice /ˈɒfɪs/

5 in a school /skuːl/

6 in a <u>fac</u>tory /ˈfæktəri/

7 at home /həʊm/

8 in the street /striːt/

b Cover the phrases. Look at the photos. Say the phrases.

c Ask and answer with a partner.

Where does a doctor work?) (*In a hospital.*

d Where do <u>you</u> work or study?
I _____.

🔙 p.36

A typical day

a 🔊 **6.14** Listen and repeat the phrases.

IN THE MORNING

1. get up /get ʌp/

2. have <u>break</u>fast
/hæv ˈbrekfəst/

3. have a <u>show</u>er
/hæv ə ˈʃaʊə/

4. go to work
/gəʊ tə wɜːk/
(by bus, train, car, etc.)

5. have a <u>coffee</u>
/hæv ə ˈkɒfi/

IN THE AFTERNOON

6. have lunch /hæv lʌntʃ/

7. <u>fin</u>ish work
/ˈfɪnɪʃ wɜːk/

8. go home /gəʊ həʊm/

9. go <u>shopping</u>
/gəʊ ˈʃɒpɪŋ/

10. go to the gym
/gəʊ tə ðə dʒɪm/

IN THE EVENING

11. make <u>dinn</u>er
/meɪk ˈdɪnə/

12. have <u>dinn</u>er
/hæv ˈdɪnə/

13. do <u>house</u>work
/duː ˈhaʊswɜːk/

14. watch TV
/wɒtʃ tiːˈviː/

15. have a bath
/hæv ə bɑːθ/

16. go to bed
/gəʊ tə bed/

🔎 **make** and **do**
make dinner / coffee **BUT** **do** housework,
do homework

go with **to** and **the**
go **to the** gym, go **to the** cinema
go **to** work, go **to** school, go **to** bed
go home **NOT** go to home

---

b 🔊 **6.15** Listen and point to the picture.

〉) *Lisa has lunch at one o'clock.* (*Picture six.*

ACTIVATION In pairs, describe Lisa's day. Say the times where there are clocks.

She gets up at a quarter to seven. 〉) (*She has breakfast.*

🔵 p.38

 **Go online** to review the vocabulary for each lesson

Common verb phrases 2

1 FREE TIME

a 🔊 **7.4** Listen and repeat the verbs and verb phrases.

go out /gəʊ aʊt/ (at night)

play compu**ter** games /pleɪ kəm'pjuːtə geɪmz/

do sport /duː spɔːt/

go to the beach /gəʊ tə ðə biːtʃ/ (the ci**nema**, the **theatre**, etc.)

stay at home /steɪ ət həʊm/

play tennis /pleɪ 'tenɪs/

walk /wɔːk/ (in the **moun**tains)

play the pi**a**no /pleɪ ðə pi'ænəʊ/

swim /swɪm/

meet friends /miːt frendz/

relax /rɪ'læks/

travel /'trævl/

🔍 **meet**

meet a person for the first time | meet at the station | meet friends after work

---

b Cover the words. Look at the photos. Say the verbs or phrases.

ACTIVATION Work in pairs. Make true sentences with *sometimes* or *never*.

I sometimes go to the cinema.) (*I never play computer games.*

2 TRAVELLING

🔊 **9.5** Listen and repeat the verb phrases.

book tickets /bʊk 'tɪkɪts/

pack a suitcase /pæk ə 'suːtkeɪs/

leave the house /liːv ðə haʊs/

carry a suitcase /'kæri ə 'suːtkeɪs/

wear sunglasses /weə 'sʌnglɑːsɪz/

get a taxi (a train, a bus) /get ə 'tæksi/

wait for a flight /weɪt fɔː ə flaɪt/

rent a car /rent ə kɑː/

arrive at a ho**tel** /ə'raɪv aet ə həʊ'tel/ (in a city)

stay in a ho**tel** /steɪ ɪn ə həʊ'tel/

phone home /fəʊn həʊm/

buy presents /baɪ 'preznts/

ACTIVATION Cover the verb phrases. Look at the photos. Work in pairs. Ask *What's she doing? What's he doing? What are they doing?*

🔗 p.55

Months and ordinal numbers

1 MONTHS

a 🔊 7.21 Listen and repeat the months.

January /'dʒænjuəri/

February /'februəri/

March /mɑːtʃ/

April /'eɪprəl/

May /meɪ/

June /dʒuːn/

July /dʒuˈlaɪ/

August /'ɔːgəst/

September /sepˈtembə/

October /ɒkˈtəʊbə/

November /nəʊˈvembə/

December /dɪˈsembə/

🔍 **Months begin with a CAPITAL letter.**
January **NOT** january

ACTIVATION Cover the months and look at JAN, FEB, etc. Say the months. ⬅ p.46

2 ORDINAL NUMBERS

a 🔊 7.23 Listen and repeat the ordinal numbers from 1st–20th.

1st first /fɜːst/
2nd second /'sekənd/
3rd third /θɜːd/
4th fourth /fɔːθ/
5th fifth /fɪfθ/
6th sixth /sɪksθ/
7th seventh /'sevnθ/
8th eighth /eɪtθ/
9th ninth /naɪnθ/
10th tenth /tenθ/
11th eleventh /ɪˈlevnθ/
12th twelfth /twelfθ/
13th thirteenth /θɜːˈtiːnθ/
14th fourteenth /fɔːˈtiːnθ/
15th fifteenth /fɪfˈtiːnθ/
16th sixteenth /sɪksˈtiːnθ/
17th seventeenth /ˌsevnˈtiːnθ/
18th eighteenth /eɪˈtiːnθ/
19th nineteenth /naɪnˈtiːnθ/
20th twentieth /'twentiəθ/

b 🔊 7.24 Now listen and repeat the ordinal numbers from 21st–31st.

21st twenty-first /ˌtwenti ˈfɜːst/
22nd twenty-second /ˌtwenti ˈsekənd/
23rd twenty-third /ˌtwenti ˈθɜːd/
24th twenty-fourth /ˌtwenti ˈfɔːθ/
25th twenty-fifth /ˌtwenti ˈfɪfθ/
26th twenty-sixth /ˌtwenti ˈsɪksθ/
27th twenty-seventh /ˌtwenti ˈsevnθ/
28th twenty-eighth /ˌtwenti ˈeɪtθ/
29th twenty-ninth /ˌtwenti ˈnaɪnθ/
30th thirtieth /'θɜːtiəθ/
31st thirty-first /ˌθɜːti ˈfɜːst/

ACTIVATION Cover the words and look at the numbers (1st, 2nd, etc.). Say the numbers. ⬅ p.46

🔄 **Go online** to review the vocabulary for each lesson

Activities

🔊 **8.13** Listen and repeat the words and phrases.

buying clothes /ˈbaɪɪŋ kləʊðz /

camping /ˈkæmpɪŋ

cooking /ˈkʊkɪŋ /

cycling /ˈsaɪklɪŋ/

doing yoga /ˈduːɪŋ jəʊgə/

eating out /ˈiːtɪŋ aʊt/

flying /ˈflaɪɪŋ/

going for a walk /ˈgəʊɪŋ fə ə wɔːk/

going to the cinema /ˈgəʊɪŋ tə ðə ˈsɪnəmə/

painting /ˈpeɪntɪŋ/

reading /ˈriːdɪŋ /

running /ˈrʌnɪŋ/

shopping /ˈʃɒpɪŋ/

singing /ˈsɪŋɪŋ/

sleeping /ˈsliːpɪŋ/

swimming /ˈswɪmɪŋ/

travelling /ˈtrævəlɪŋ/

watching TV series /wɒtʃɪŋ ˈtiː viː sɪəriːz/

ACTIVATION Cover the activities and look at the photos. Say the activities.

🔙 p.50

Clothes

a 9.14 Listen and repeat the clothes words.

1 sweater /ˈswetə/
2 T-shirt /ˈtiː ʃɜːt/
3 shirt /ʃɜːt/
4 trousers /ˈtraʊzəz/
5 jeans /dʒiːnz/
6 shorts /ʃɔːts/
7 suit /suːt/
8 dress /dres/
9 skirt /skɜːt/
10 coat /kəʊt/
11 jacket /ˈdʒækɪt/
12 socks /sɒks/
13 trainers /ˈtreɪnəz/
14 shoes /ʃuːz/
15 hat /hæt/
16 cap /kæp/

b Cover the words. Look at the photos. Say the words.

ACTIVATION Work in pairs. Ask about other students: *What's he wearing? What's she wearing?*

p.57

1
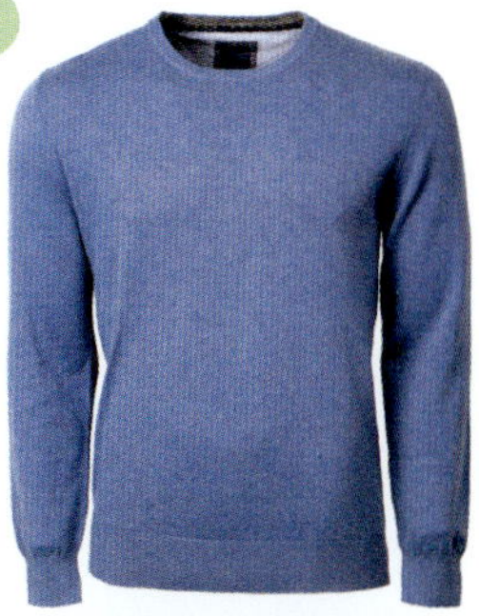
2
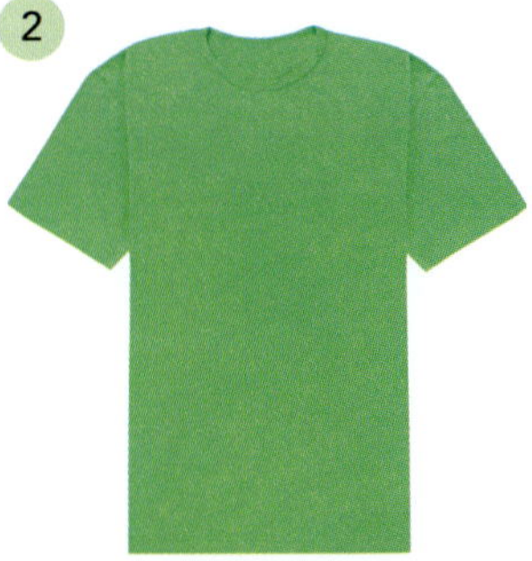
3
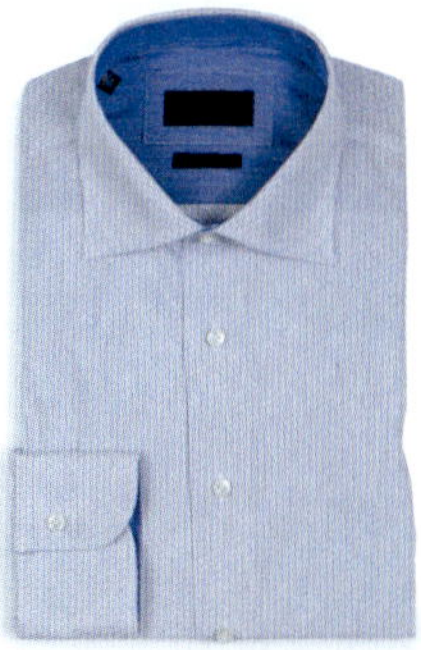
4
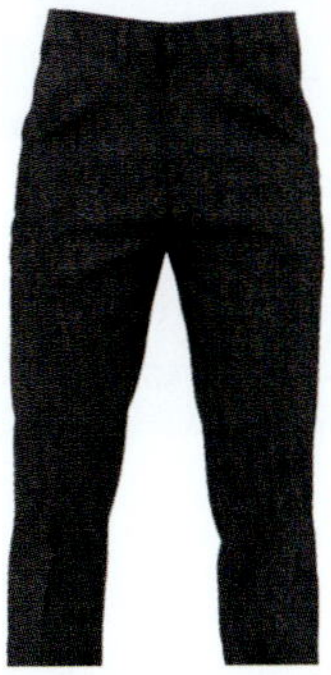
5
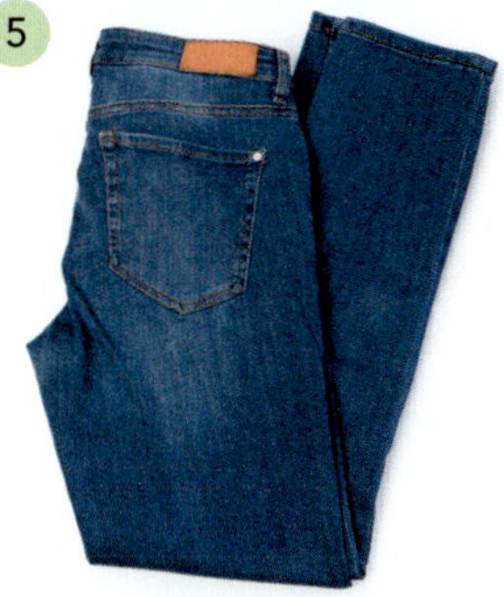
6
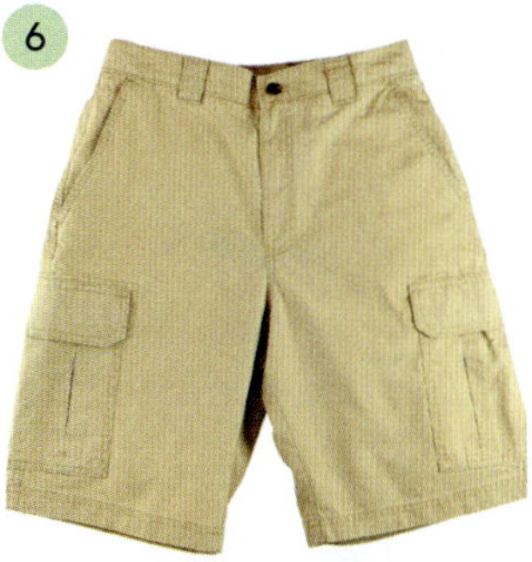
7
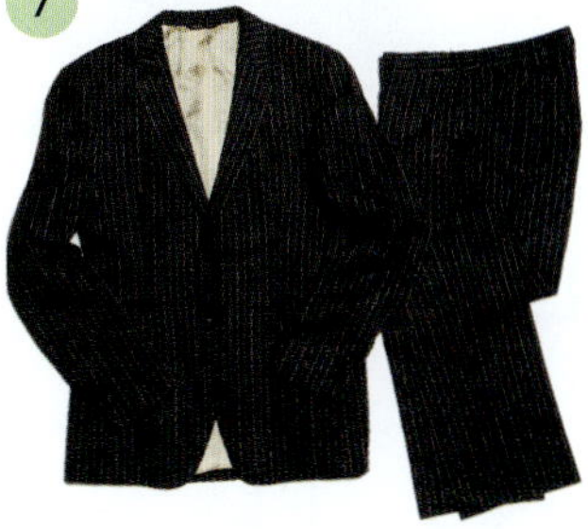
8
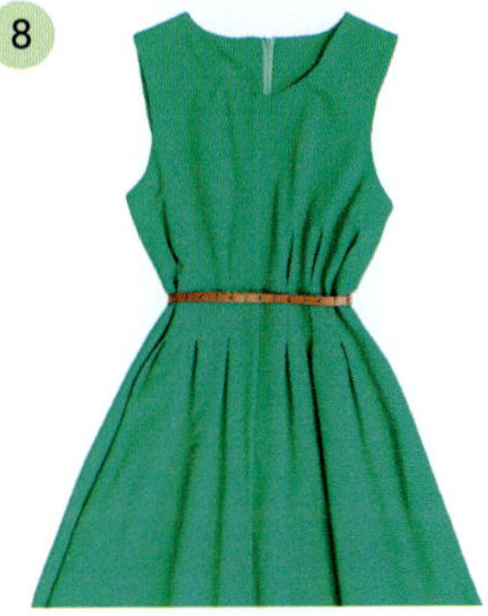
9
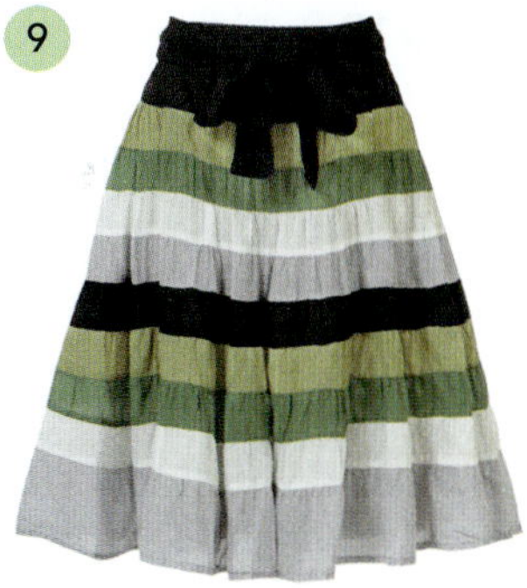
10
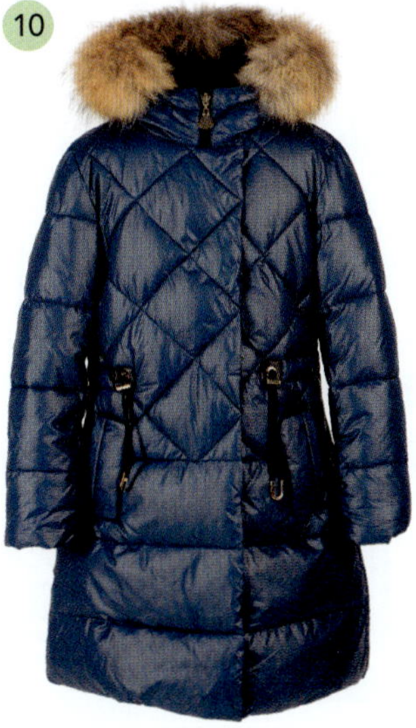
11
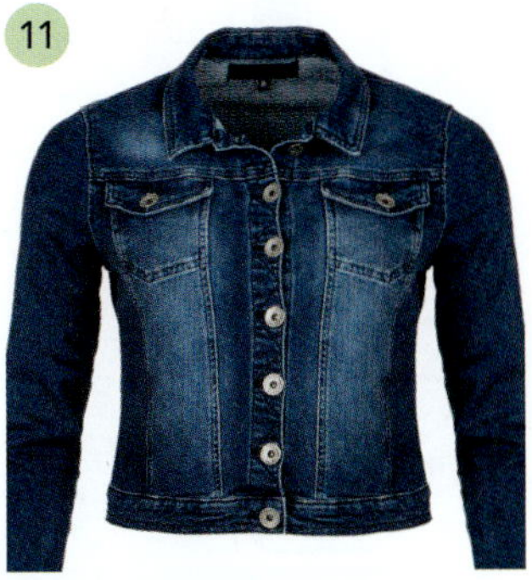
12
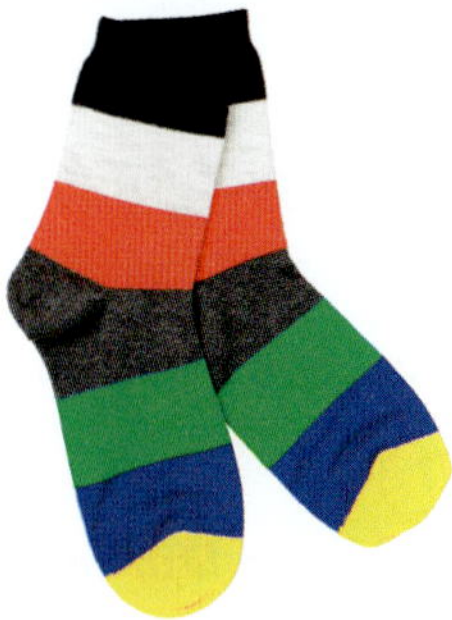
13
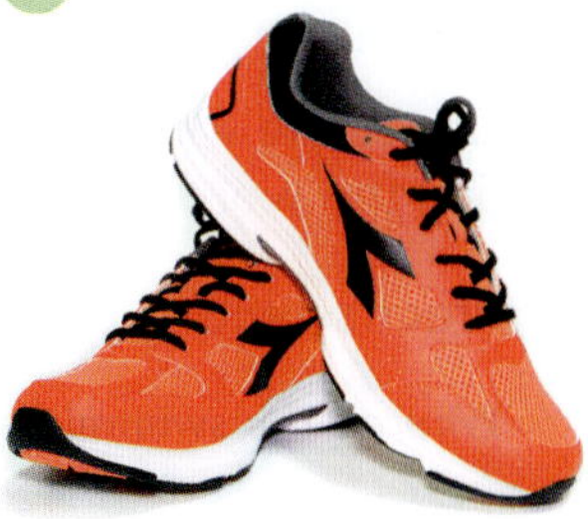
14
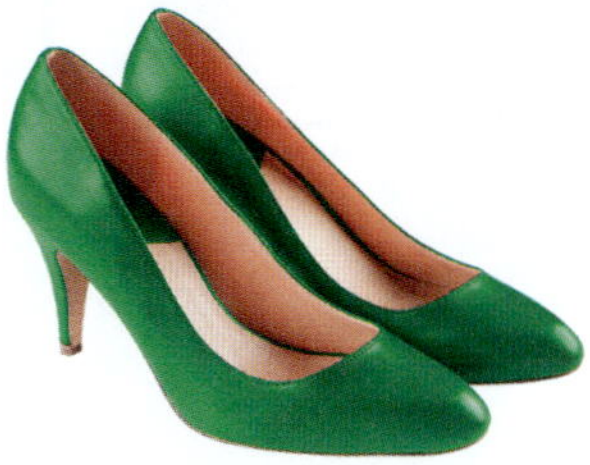
15
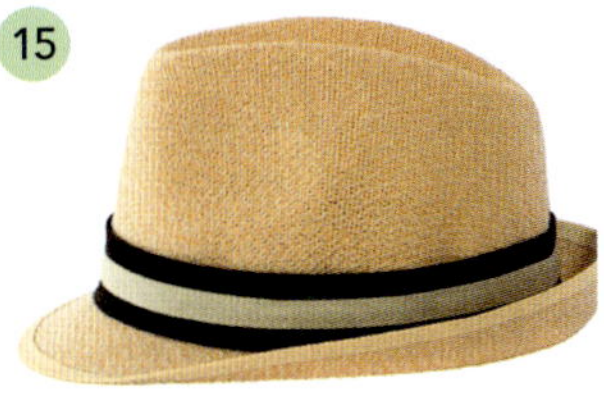
16
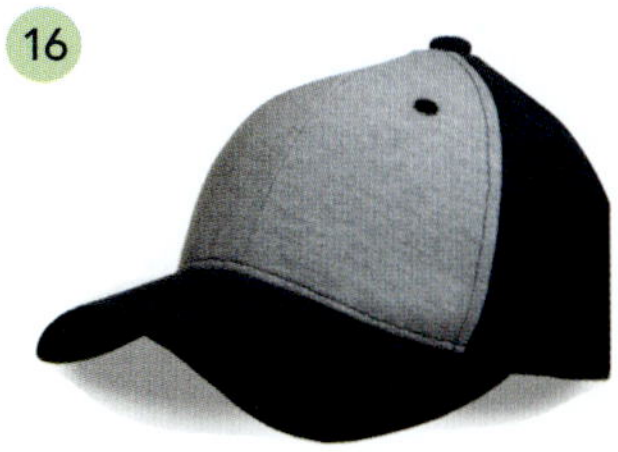

Go online to review the vocabulary for each lesson

Hotels

1 IN A HOTEL ROOM

a 🔊 **10.2** Listen and repeat the words.

1 a bed /bed/
2 a pillow /'pɪləʊ/
3 a table /'teɪbl/
4 a lamp /læmp/
5 a light /laɪt/
6 a remote control /rɪˌməʊt kən'trəʊl/
7 the floor /flɔː/
8 the bathroom /'bɑːθruːm/
9 a bath /bɑːθ/
10 a shower /'ʃaʊə/
11 a towel /'taʊəl/
12 a cupboard /'kʌbəd/

b Cover the words. Look at the picture. Say the words.

2 IN A HOTEL

a 🔊 **10.3** Listen and repeat the words.

1 a swimming pool /'swɪmɪŋ puːl/
2 a spa /spɑː/
3 toilets /'tɔɪləts/
4 a restaurant /'restrɒnt/
5 a bar /bɑː/
6 a gym /dʒɪm/
7 a lift /lɪft/
8 a gift shop /'gɪft ʃɒp/
9 reception /rɪ'sepʃn/
10 a garden /'gɑːdn/
11 a car park /'kɑː pɑːk/

b Cover the words. Look at the picture. Say the words.

c Practise with a partner. Ask and answer.

Where's the swimming pool?

It's on the fifth floor.

🔍 **ground floor**
the floor of a building at street level

⬅ p.60

Words and phrases to learn

1A 🔊 1.15

Hello.
Hi.
What's your name?
Nice to meet you.

A cappuccino, please.
A tea.
Yes.
No.
OK.
Thanks.
Sorry.
Just a minute.

Goodbye. / Bye.
See you on Friday.
See you tomorrow.

1B 🔊 1.31

Where are you from?
I'm from Spain.
Where's Izmir?
I think it's in Turkey.
It's a nice city.

I don't know.
Very good.
Wow!

2A 🔊 2.12

Excuse me.
Are they free?
Are you on holiday?
We're on business.
What's that?
Have a nice day!
It's a beautiful city.
tourists
dogs
over there

2B 🔊 2.27

Who's he?
How old is he?
He's very good-looking.

How are you?
I'm fine.
This is Alex.
That's my bus.
This is my bus stop.

What class are you in?
What's your phone number?
See you later.

a bedroom
a kitchen
a garden

big
small

in the south of England

3A 🔊 3.9

Oh no!
Where's my phone?
Where are my glasses?

What is it?
What are they?

I think it's an ID card.
I think they're keys.

What's in your bag?
I have two credit cards.

3B 🔊 3.17

How much is this mug?
How much are these key
   rings?
They're twenty pounds.
A T-shirt, please.

Is this your phone?
Thank you very much.
You're welcome.

souvenirs
here
there

4A 🔊 4.12

Come in.
Be good.
Let's order pizza.

on the table
in my phone

Mum
Dad
a babysitter

What a lovely card!
Can I see?
I remember.
perhaps

4B 🔊 4.24

sir
madam

an electric car
a sports car

easy to park
perfect

in her (my, your,…) opinion
Is the car for you?
I prefer this red car.
I love it!
Come with me.

a museum
a village
a motorbike
famous

5A 🔊 5.10

a scientist
a doctor

sometimes
usually

I'm not hungry.
early
healthy
traditional
important
different
favourite

in a café
at home
at work

soup
green tea
toast
a lot of (fruit)

5B 🔊 5.20

a writer
a taxi driver
a British (American)
   company
a flight
traffic
a gate

at university
at school

Do you want fish or pasta?
How's your pasta?
I need to go to the toilet.
What time do we arrive?
Keep the change.
Can I see your passport and
   boarding pass, please?
What a nice surprise!

6A 🔊 6.11

What does she do?
Where does he teach?
She's a journalist.
She doesn't wear glasses.
Her hair's blonde.
He's married to Lisa.

Great to see you.
intelligent
How awful!
I love your shoes.

a barman
a banker
customers
dishes
a multinational company
meetings

Why? Because…

6B 🔊 6.19

Are you a morning person?
What time do you get up?
At eight o'clock.
He gets up at about 9.30.
feel tired

on the way to work
after work
every morning
then

a tour guide
an apartment
the subway
an omelette

It's delicious.

7A 🔊 7.9

per cent
do the same thing
fun
exciting
at home

a pub
a supermarket
a football fan

it depends
more or less
except
definitely

7B 🔊 7.20

a film director
an actor
a scene
kiss

Be quiet.
Don't cry.
Don't move.
Don't say anything.
I don't remember.
What about?

next to
nothing

8A 🔊 8.12

a driving licence
a theory test
a practical test
a driving instructor

take a test
pass
fail
learn to drive
start the car

nervous
Total disaster!

I'm free on Monday.
Yes, of course.

8B 🔊 8.18

horrible
peaceful
frightened
alone
at parties
concentrate
very loudly

9A 🔊 9.9

a living room
the box office
traffic
noise
jacket
hear
darling

half an hour
towards
outside

Are you sure?
Have a good day.
See you in 20 minutes.

9B 🔊 9.18

a boss
work experience

wash the dishes
repair something
serve breakfast
work hard
clean a room
make changes
make friends

broken
tired
surprised

10A 🔊 10.10

a tourist destination
the coast
an island
a lake
a castle
a visitor
a bar
a day trip
a boat trip
a monster
a room for tonight
a great view
on the second floor
Enjoy your stay.

10B 🔊 10.18

a robbery
a bank
a suspect
a detective

yesterday
yesterday afternoon
last night
last Friday night

secret
strong
together

the 15th century

lock
store rooms
a building
a luxury hotel

11A 🔊 11.8

a designer
a National Park
public transport
a trumpet
a sports club

blueberries
abroad
organic
cheaper than

decide
invite
offer
miss
visit
pick
return

11B 🔊 11.16

an early flight
an exam
a noise
eyes
an operation
a soldier
a special day
the 21st century

pretty
shave
enjoy
go to hospital
ask somebody to marry you
get married
have a party

I'm back.
How was your day?

12A 🔊 12.12

a platform
a nice smell
classical music
a message
tickets for a concert
a concert hall
a seat
full
exchange
turn on a light

That's interesting.
Time to go.

Regular and irregular verbs

COMMON REGULAR VERBS

answer /'ɑːnsə/	answered /'ɑːnsəd/
arrive /ə'raɪv/	arrived /ə'raɪvd/
ask /ɑːsk/	asked /ɑːskt/
book /bʊk/	booked /bʊkt/
carry /'kæri/	carried /'kærid/
change /tʃeɪndʒ/	changed /tʃeɪndʒd/
check in /tʃek 'ɪn/	checked in /tʃekt 'ɪn/
clean /kliːn/	cleaned /kliːnd/
close /kləʊz/	closed /kləʊzd/
cook /kʊk/	cooked /kʊkt/
cry /kraɪ/	cried /kraɪd/
decide /dɪ'saɪd/	decided /dɪ'saɪdɪd/
finish /'fɪnɪʃ/	finished /'fɪnɪʃt/
hate /heɪt/	hated /'heɪtɪd/
help /help/	helped /helpt/
invite /ɪn'vaɪt/	invited /ɪn'vaɪtɪd/
learn /lɜːn/	learned /lɜːnd/
like /laɪk/	liked /laɪkt/
listen /'lɪsn/	listened /'lɪsnd/
live /lɪv/	lived /lɪvd/
look /lʊk/	looked /lʊkt/
love /lʌv/	loved /lʌvd/
miss /mɪs/	missed /mɪst/
move /muːv/	moved /muːvd/
need /niːd/	needed /'niːdɪd/
offer /'ɒfə/	offered /'ɒfəd/
open /'əʊpən/	opened /'əʊpənd/
pack /pæk/	packed /pækt/
paint /peɪnt/	painted /'peɪntɪd/
park /pɑːk/	parked /pɑːkt/
pass /pɑːs/	passed /pɑːst/
phone /fəʊn/	phoned /fəʊnd/
play /pleɪ/	played /pleɪd/
rain /reɪn/	rained /reɪnd/
relax /rɪ'læks/	relaxed /rɪ'lækst/
rent /rent/	rented /'rentɪd/
snow /snəʊ/	snowed /snəʊd/
start /stɑːt/	started /'stɑːtɪd/
stay /steɪ/	stayed /steɪd/
stop /stɒp/	stopped /stɒpt/
study /'stʌdi/	studied /'stʌdid/
talk /tɔːk/	talked /tɔːkt/
travel /'trævl/	travelled /'trævld/
turn /tɜːn/	turned /tɜːnd/
use /juːz/	used /juːzd/
wait /weɪt/	waited /'weɪtɪd/
walk /wɔːk/	walked /wɔːkt/
want /wɒnt/	wanted /'wɒntɪd/
wash /wɒʃ/	washed /wɒʃd/
watch /wɒtʃ/	watched /wɒtʃt/
work /wɜːk/	worked /wɜːkt/

COMMON IRREGULAR VERBS

be /biː/	
am /æm/ / is /ɪz/	was /wɒz/
are /ɑː/	were /wɜː/
buy /baɪ/	bought /bɔːt/
do /duː/	did /dɪd/
get /get/	got /gɒt/
go /gəʊ/	went /went/
have /hæv/	had /hæd/
leave /liːv/	left /left/
say /seɪ/	said /sed/
see /siː/	saw /sɔː/
send /send/	sent /sent/
sit /sɪt/	sat /sæt/
tell /tel/	told /təʊld/
write /raɪt/	wrote /rəʊt/

Vowel sounds

		usual spelling	! but also
fish	i	Italy six is it film window	English women gym
tree	ee ea e	three meet please read she we	people key
cat	a	bag thanks man black bad that	
car	ar a	are park fast father afternoon	
clock	o	not from sorry stop coffee	what watch want
horse	or al aw	short important tall football draw	water four
bull	u oo	full sugar good book look cook	woman could
boot	oo u* ew	too food excuse blue new	two you juice beautiful
computer	Many different spellings, always unstressed. sister actor famous about policeman		
bird	er ir ur	person verb thirsty girl nurse Turkey	work word world
egg	e	spell ten seven twenty Mexico	friend breakfast bread
up	u	umbrella number brush husband but	son brother young

		usual spelling	! but also
train	a* ai ay	name late email Spain day say	eight they great
phone	o* oa	open close no hello coat	window
bike	i* y igh	I Hi nice bye my night right	buy
owl	ou ow	out house pound sound town down	
boy	oi oy	toilet noise boyfriend enjoy	
ear	eer ere ear	beer here we're near year	really idea cereal
chair	air ere	airport repair where there	their careful
tourist	A very unusual sound. euro Europe sure plural		
/i/	A sound between /ɪ/ and /iː/. Consonant + y at the end of words is pronounced /i/. happy angry hungry		
/u/	An unusual sound. usually situation education		

* especially before consonant + e

 short vowels  long vowels diphthongs

Consonant sounds

		usual spelling		! but also
parrot	p	paper Poland sleep top		
	pp	opposite happy		
bag	b	board British remember job		
	bb	hobby		
key	c	colour credit card		chemist's
	k	look coke		
	ck	back clock		
girl	g	go green big blog		
	gg	eggs		
flower	f	fifteen Friday wife		
	ph	photo phone		
	ff	office different		
vase	v	TV very have live seven five		of
tie	t	time tell start late		liked finished
	tt	letter butter		
dog	d	did drink study good		played cried
	dd	address middle		
snake	s	sit stand		science
	ss	Swiss actress		
	ce/ci	nice city		
zebra	z	zero Brazil		
	s	bags cars husband easy		
shower	sh	shop she Spanish finish		sugar sure Russia
	ti	information reservation (ti + on)		
television	si (+ on) revision			usually garage

		usual spelling		! but also
thumb	th	thing think tenth birthday month Thursday		
mother	th	the father this their that with		
chess	ch	children lunch		
	tch	watch match		
	t (+ure)	picture		
jazz	j	Japan juice job		gym page
	dge	bridge		
leg	l	lamp listen plan table		
	ll	small umbrella		
right	r	red rice problem street		write wrong
	rr	terrible married		
witch	w	watch twenty word we		one
	wh	what white where		
yacht	y	yellow your yes you		
	before u	student university		
monkey	m	museum Monday September come		
	mm	summer swimming		
nose	n	nine never men fine		know
	nn	beginner dinner		
singer	ng	thing single doing going playing wrong		think thank
house	h	hello hi how he have holiday		who

☐ unvoiced   ☐ voiced

Go online to watch the Sound Bank videos

OXFORD
UNIVERSITY PRESS

Great Clarendon Street, Oxford, OX2 6DP,
United Kingdom

Oxford University Press is a department of the
University of Oxford. It furthers the University's
objective of excellence in research, scholarship,
and education by publishing worldwide. Oxford
is a registered trade mark of Oxford University
Press in the UK and in certain other countries

© Oxford University Press 2019

The moral rights of the author have been asserted

First published in 2019

2024

12

No unauthorized photocopying

ISBN: 978 0 19 402992 6

Printed in China

This book is printed on paper from certified
and well-managed sources.

ACKNOWLEDGEMENTS

Back cover photograph: Oxford University Press building/David
Fisher

*The authors would like to thank all the teachers and students round the
world whose feedback has helped us to shape English File.*

The authors would also like to thank: all those at Oxford University
Press (both in Oxford and around the world) and the design
team who have contributed their skills and ideas to producing
this course.

*Finally very special thanks from Clive to Maria Angeles, Lucia, and Eric,
and from Christina to Cristina, for all their support and encouragement.
Christina would also like to thank her children Joaquin, Marco, and
Krysia for their constant inspiration.*

*The publisher and authors are very grateful to the following who have
provided personal stories and/or photographs:* Hannah Donat and
Dominic Latham-Koenig

*The publisher and authors would also like to thank the following for
their invaluable feedback on the materials:* Magdalena Muszyńska,
Brian Brennan, Krysia Mabbott, Dagmara Łata, Elif Barbaros,
Zahra Bilides, Kenny McDonnell, Rosa María Iglesias Traviesas,
Yolanda Calpe, Ana María Vallejo Guijarro, Patricia Ares

Sources: www.express.co.uk; www.dailymail.co.uk/femail/

*Although every effort has been made to trace and contact copyright
holders before publication, this has not been possible in some cases. We
apologize for any apparent infringement of copyright and if notified, the
publisher will be pleased to rectify any errors or omissions at the earliest
opportunity.*

*We would also like to thank the following for permission to reproduce the
following photographs:* 123RF pp.18 (one umbrella/Tatiana
Popova), (four pencils/Liubov Shirokova), (two laptops/zentilia),
19 (E/Hemant Mehta); Alamy pp.9 (3/richard sowersby), (5/Steve
Barnett), (7/World Discovery), (11/Roger Bamber), 10 (6/
Shotshop GmbH), 12 (1/Michael Willis), (2/B Christopher), (3/
Richard Sharrocks), (4/Martin Lee), 19 (A/Photoinke), (12/Paul
Herbert), 20 (stall/James Clarke Images), 22 (£10 GBP/Nick
Fielding), (€10 Euros/Iakov Filimonov), ($10 US/Joe Sohm/
Visions of America, LLC), 26 (Tizzy/Simon Stuart-Miller),
27 (films/Everett Collection Inc), 34 (smartphone inset in A/
Mike Abbott), (wristwatch repeated/musk), 45 (Alien
Prometheus/AF archive), (Michael Fassbender/AF archive),
46 (Legionaries/Rolf Richardson), 48 (damaged car/Juha
Jarvinen), (driving instruction car/Mark Waugh), 49 (6/
Beaconstox), (8/Adrian Weston), 53 (Belfast/Chris Hill/National
Geographic Creative), 56 (fixing oven/Andriy Popov), 57 (Fat
Face store/fc2/picturesbyrob), 59 (pizza/Colin Cadle
Photography), (football/Sergio Azenha), 60 (Loch Ness monster/
AF archive), 62 (AF archive), 64 (suit jacket/Oleksiy
Maksymenko Photography), 65 (watching tv/Frank Sanchez),
69 (boy shaving/Nick Moore), (cleaning shoes/ton koene),
(cyclist/Frank Bienewald), 77 (woman on camel/age fotostock),
78 (10 Swatch/Richard Levine), 80 (museum/Alex Segre), 82 (10
Swatch/Richard Levine), 117 (3/blickwinkel), (5/JLImages), (7/AF
archive), (10/View Pictures Ltd), (13/Prisma Bildagentur AG),
121 (Colours 6/Jeffrey Blackler), (Colours 8/Oleksiy
Maksymenko Photography), (Adjectives 9/Jeffrey Blackler),
122 (sandwich/Barry Mason), (water/Gerhard Beneken/doc-
stock), 123 (TV/Picture Partners), (drink tea/sebastiano volponi/
MARKA), (bank/Image Source Plus), 124 (police officers/Janine
Wiedel Photolibrary), (restaurant/Andrew Twort), (office/
Hufton + Crow/View Pictures Ltd), (school/Art Directors & TRIP),
(factory/Jim West), 126 (Travelling 12/Juice Images), (Free Time
2/Kevin Britland), (Free Time 11/Jeff Morgan 01), (Travelling 6/
Terese Loeb Kreuzer), (Travelling 7/Peter Titmuss), (Travelling 8/
Kumar Sriskandan), (Travelling 9/Jeff Greenberg), 128 (9/
Keenretail); Courtesy of David Clarke p.56 (wearing a suit);
Courtesy of The Craigdarroch Inn p.60 (bedroom); Hannah
Donat p.38 (Hannah and Kit); Getty Images pp.8 (2/Onoky -
Fabrice Lerouge), (Caetano Veloso/Damian Dopacio/AFP), (Lila
Downs/Omar Vega/LatinContent Editorial), 9 (1/Joey Foley/Getty
Images Entertainment), (2/Jupiterimages/The Image Bank), (4/
Egyptian), (10/Jon Furniss/WireImage), (12/Gustavo Caballero/
Getty Images Entertainment), 13 (1/Jerod Harris/Getty Images
Entertainment), (4/Jim Spellman/WireImage), 16 (pen/Donald
Erickson/Collection E+), 17 (Mark/NicolasMcComber/E+),
28 (wallet/Creative Crop), 29 (Jeremy Fisher and family/Philip
and Karen Smith Collection/Photographer's Choice RF), (Claire
and her sisters/Westend61), 30 (Sakura/Tadamasa Taniguchi),
(coffee in office/Gregor Schuster), 35 (tired/Christopher Hope-
Fitch), (hungry/John Lund/Marc Romanelli/Blend Images), (hot/
Cultura/Chris Whitehead), (thirsty/Peter Cade/Iconica), 36 (1/
Chris Condon/US PGA Tour), (3/Frederic Lucano/The Image
Bank), 42 (Polly and Andrew/Antenna), 46 (JK Rowling/Dave J
Hogan/Getty Images Europe), 49 (2/Bloomberg via Getty
Images), (3/Digital Vision/Riou), (4/Ibusca), (5/Oliver Strewe/
Lonely Planet Images), (9/Jung Yeon-Je/AFP), 52 (couple on
plane/fStop Images/Halfdark), (artist/Caiaimage/Rafal Rodzoch),
57 (1/Gary Alvis), (Sandra/Juanmonino), 60 (Loch Ness/Andreas
Strauss/Look-foto), 64 (shoes/Stuart Burr), 65 (balcony/Ferad
Zyulkyarov/Moment), 66 (plane/Bloomberg), (pub/Roy
MehtaTaxi), 78 (2/Visual China Group), (3/Giuseppe Cacace/
AFP), (4/Alex Davies/FilmMagic), (5/Michael Melford/National
Geographic Magazines), (6/Victor Virgile/Gamma-Rapho), (7/
Bloomberg), (9/Jose Perez Gegundez/Gamma-Rapho), (9/
Bloomberg), 80 (restaurant/Andrew Holt Collection/Photographer's),
82 (reused from p.78) 117 (2/Luis Castaneda Inc), (6/Izzet
Keribar), 120 (People 1/Stefka Pavlova/Moment Open), (People
2/Gen Umekita), 121 (Colours 9/Nikada/E+), (Adjectives 2/
Michael Melford/Photographer's Choice), (Adjectives 5/Car
Culture), (Adjectives 6/Ken Ishii/Getty Images AsiaPac),
123 (radio/Frontdoor Images/Stone), (dog/Rafael Elias), (cats/
Cultura/Zak Kendal), (broken down car/Rhienna Cutler/E+),
124 (journalist/Max Mumby/Indigo), (shop assistant/
Bloomberg), (receptionist/Frederic Lucano/The Image Bank),
(factory worker/Monty Rakusen/Cultura), (cab driver/
Jupiterimages/Photolibrary), (department store/Bloomberg),
(desk at home/Westend61), 126 (Free Time 1/Blend Images/Jose
Luis Pelaez Inc), (Free Time 4/Robert Daly/Ojo Images), (Free
Time 5/Morsa Images), (Free Time 8/Stock4B), (Travelling 2/
Andersen Ross/Blend Images), (Travelling 11/Emma Innocenti/
Taxi), 128 (14/Philippe Lissac/Godong/Corbis Documentary), (17/vgajic/
E+); Phil Hill @ United National Photographers p.56 (David
Clarke working in hotel); iStockphoto p.42 (man washing up/
Graham Oliver); Christina Latham-Koenig pp.37; Dominic
Latham-Koening pp.66 (Dominic and family), 66 (Dominic's
house), 67; Reproduced by permission of Oxford University
Press from Oxford Essential Dictionary © Oxford University
Press 2012 p.16 (dictionary); Reproduced by permission of
Oxford University Press; p.66 cover of SPLAT! (2017) By Jon
Burgerman and cover of Mr Bunny's Chocolate Factory (2017)
by Elys Dolan; Oxford University Press pp.18 (one pencil), 22 (50
cents), 40 (bread), (orange juice), 59 (sandwich), 117, 117 (9),
120 (Family 1 & 2), (Family 7-8/Image Source/Getty Images),
121 (Adjectives 15), (Adjectives 16), 129 (suit); Oxford University
Press\Alamy pp.16 (whiteboard/RTimages), (door/Dmytro
Grankin), 22 (50 pence/Images), 35 (cold/XiXinXing), 49 (1/Perry
van Munster), (7/Esa Hiltula), 52 (camping/Stockbroker), 57 (3/
Dudley Wood), 59 (coffee/Piotr Skubisz), 64 (suit trousers/
Creative Control), 84 (couple/Juice Images), (opening times/Jack
Carey), 86 (family), 116 (Sean Gladwell), 117 (4/Jan Tadeusz), (8/
Sean Pavone), 120 (People 6/Image Source), (Family 3-6/D.
Hurst), (Family 11-12/Ojo Images Ltd), 121 (Colours 3/Marek
Kosmal), (Colours 7/Nalinratana Phiyanalinmat), (Colours 10/
Artem Merzlenko), (Adjectives 10/Picturebank), 122 (yoghurt/
FoodFood), (milk/Valentyn Volkov), (orange juice/imageBroker),
(man drinking/Mint Images), 123 (flat/UpperCut Images),
(breakfast/UpperCut Images), (newspaper/Juice Images), (speak
English/Andres Rodriguez), (want coffee/Image Source Plus),
(polystyrene cup/Judith Collins), (classes/Cathy Topping),
124 (nurse/OJO Images Ltd), (hospital/Zoonar GmbH),
126 (Travelling 10/Hybrid Images/Image Source Salsa); Oxford
University Press\Corbis pp.17 (Bianca), 122 (vegetables),
123 (fast food); Oxford University Press\DAJ p.122 (tea); Oxford
University Press\Photodisc p.22 (25 cents); Oxford University
Press\Photolibrary pp.8 (1), 22 (25 cents), 59 (coke), 87,
122 (eggs), 124 (doctor); Oxford University Press\Shutterstock
pp.18 (picture frame/pixelheadphoto digitalskillet), 27 (houses/
Ewelina Wachala), 41 (Japanese food/bonshan),
119 (newspaper), 122 (salad/Kuttelvaserova Stuchelova); REX\
Shutterstock pp.19 (D/Pablo Martinez Monsivais/AP),
45 (Charlize Theron/Scott Free Prod/20th Century Fox/Kobal),
(Sigourney Weaver/Denis Cameron), (Alien (original)/20th
Century Fox/Kobal), (AlienCovenant/Rob Latour), 46 (The Lord
of the Rings/New Line/Kobal), (Star Wars/Lucasfilm/Fox/Kobal),
121 (Adjectives 7/Image Broker), (Adjectives 8/John O'Reilly),
128 (18 still from 'House' on TV screen/Fox-TV/Kobal);
Shutterstock pp.8 (3/bezikus), (back view couple/Kamenetskiy
Konstantin), (wall/rangizzz), (pavement/donatas1205), (poster
graphic/balabolka), 9 (6/Vereshchagin Dmitry), (8/Scharfsinn),
(9/Lev Kropotov), 10 (1/Jordan Tan), (2/chrisdorney), (3/Marija
Stojkovic), (4/Claudio Divizia), (5/Stephen Coburn), (7/Sergio
Monti Photography), (8/Jack Jelly), 13 (2/Waldemar Dabrowski),
(3/Dawid Lech), 16 (chair/Just2shutter), 17 (Jacek/LightField
Studios), 18 (book/Amero), (semi-closed laptop/Peter Kotoff),
(phone/RikoBest), (smiling woman/Kim Diaz), (open laptop/
Nata-Lia), (three umbrellas/Anton-Burakov), 19 (B/Atstock
Productions), (C/stockfour), (1/natushm), (2/Brilliance stock), (3/
Nitikorn Poonsiri), (4/David Baumgartner), (5/alexialex), (6/
kozirsky), (7/Jakraphong Photography), (8/Claudio Divizia), (9/
mrkornflakes), (10/akiyoko), (11/aPhoenixPhotographer),
20 (football shirt/Rabilbanimilbu), 24 (boy/list), (girl/list), (man/
list), (woman/list), 26 (car logos/Rose Carson), (Audi TT/eans),
27 (cities/segawa7), (food/Onchira Wongsiri), (restaurants/
SPhoto), (books/Billion Photos), (dogs/InBetweentheBlinks),
(photos/bepsy), 28 (umbrella/burnel1), (credit card/yablueko),
(key/Winai Tepsuttinun), (cap/Etaphop photo), (teddy/Num
LPPhoto), 30 (sandwich/gowithstock), (eggs/Africa Studio),
(tea/M. Unal Ozmen), (cheese/Nattika), (orange juice/Africa
Studio), (Marta/Kudryashova Alla), (Paulo/LightField Studios),
(Rob/Azovtsev Maksym), (coffee cup/3DMAVR), 34 (clock
graphic 1-6/Lightkite), 36 (2/wavebreakmedia), 37 (Antonio/
David Tadevosian), (Charlotte/Africa Studio), (nurse/Monkey
Business Images), (hospital background/Joachim Heng),
38 (avocado/NatashaPhoto), (bath/stocksolutions), 40 (water/
Gyvafoto), (sugar/Sea Wave), (milk/Jon Le-Bon), (cheese),
42 (woman watching tv/antoniodiaz), 46 (keyboard/Guguart),
(Fifth Avenue/Tono Balaguer), 49 (10/Richyjh), 50 (1/Mima
Antic), (2/Erin Cadigan), (3/CKp.1001), (Isabella/Twin Sails),
(William/VGstockstudio), (Angie/Taras Atamaniv), (Daniel/Dean
Drobot), (Adriana/De Repente), (Luke/Dean Drobot), 52 (cycling/
Ljupco Smokovski), (cooking/Robert Kneschke), (man with
suitcase/leolintang), (jogging/Dean Drobot), (swimming/
Suzanne Tucker), 57 (2/Karkas), (4/Chiyacat), (5/Mariyana M),
59 (salad/Christian Jung), (party/Monkey Business Images),
(concert/melis), 60 (map/Natalia Chuen), 61 (view through the
window/Alinute Silzeviciute), 63 (digital clock 7 am and 10am/
creatOR76), (digital clock 4 pm and 6.30pm/Macrovector),
(wristwatch/MarySan), (Jason's wife/Spectral-Design), 64 (dress/
Karkas), (jacket/mates), (shirt/OZaiachin), (skirt/Karkas),
(trousers/Elnur), (hat/Slavko Sereda), 65 (Jenna/Wayhome
studio), (couple/Wayhome studio), (tapas/Andreas Saldavs),
(watching tv female legs only/MarinaP), (football match on TV/
ThomasDeco), 66 (Lego helicopter/cjmacer), (mountain
landscape on booking screen/Dave Allen Photography),
(suitcases/Laborant), 68 (hallway background/Africa Studio),
69 (sky dive/Sky Antonio), (wedding/IVASHstudio), 75 (dice/
Gearstd), 77 (Petra/liseykina), 78 (1/Ratthaphong Ekariyasap), (8/
Brent Hofacker), (10 Rolex/jeafish Ping), 79 (clocks/Lightkite),
81 (charger/Passakorn sakulphan), (purse/A N D A), (iPad/nixki),
(Canadian passports/dennizn), 82 (1/Ratthaphong Ekariyasap),
(8), (10 Rolex/list), 83 (clocks/Lightkite), 85 (surprised people/
Dima Sidelnikov), 117 (1/Mark Schwettmann), (11/vvoe), (12/
Sean Pavone), (14/Luciano Mortula), (15/Critterbiz),
119 (Hungarian passport/Abihatsira Issac), (charger/Ruslan
Ivantsov), 120 (People 3/Nadino), (People 4/magedb.com),
(People 5/Andresr), (Family 9-10/wavebreakmedia), 121 (Colours
1/Elnur), (Colours 2/Pabkov), (Colours 4/Yganko), (Colours 5/
Evgen3dstudio), (Adjectives 1/pics721), (Adjectives 3/
jannoon028), (Adjectives 4/SmileStudio), (Adjectives 11/Natasha
Kramskaya), (Adjectives 12/Yuralaits Albert), (Adjectives 13/
panpote), (Adjectives 14/psirob), 122 (fish/HLPhoto), (meat/
Valentyn Volkov), (pasta/chrisbrignell), (rice/leungchopan),
(potatoes/isak55), (fruit/Africa Studio), (bread/Tim UR), (butter/
Photographee.eu), (cheese/Tim UR), (sugar/
GayvoronskayaYana), (cereal/Oliver Hoffmann), (chocolate/Yeko
Photo Studio), (coffee/Artem and Olga Sapegin), (wine/
lenetstan), (beer/Tarasyuk Igor), (woman eating/159877448),
124 (teacher/wavebreakmedia), (waiters/Dmitry Kalinovsky),
(street with police/Dutourdumonde Photography), 126 (Free
Time 3/Tono Balaguer), (Free Time 6/Andresr), (Free Time 7/
Galyna Andrushko), (Satyrenko), (Free Time 10/Lucky Business),
(Free Time 12/Teri Virbickis), (Travelling 4/Robert Kneschke),
(Travelling 5/Cookie Studio), 128 (1/ESB Professional), (2/Kiselev
Andrey Valerevich), (3/merzzie), (4/Cultura Motion), (5/I AM
NIKOM), (6/fotoinfot), (7/Akimov Igor), (8/Syda Productions), (10/
David Tadevosian), (11/Andrii Kobryn), (12/nd3000), (13/Minerva
Studio), (15/baranq), (16/Halfpoint), (18 people watching TV/
wavebreakmedia), 129 (cap/Ukki Studio), (hat/rawisoot), (coat/
elenovsky), (dress/Vlad Teodor), (jacket/Peter Versnel), (jeans/
gresei), (shirt/Elnur), (green shoes/Magdalena Wielobob), (skirt/
Karkas), (socks/ConstantinosZ), (sweater/elenovsky), (T-shirt/
Iasha), (trainers/BornRichjapan), (grey trousers/demidoff),
(shorts/windu); YRS www.your-reflection.co.uk p.60 (exterior
The Craigdarroch Inn)

Pronunciation chart artwork by: Ellis Nadler

Illustrations by: Amber Day/Illustration Ltd. pp.12, 13, 36; Jo Bird/
Jelly London p.44 (illustrated background), 70-71 (map), 81, 85;
Stephen Collins pp.125, 130; Clementine Hope/NB.Illustration
Ltd. pp.14 (illustrated background), 54, 55, 61 (illustrated
backgrounds), 80 & 84 (bedrooms); Laura Perez/Anna Goodson
Illustration Agency pp.32-33, 64; Claire Rollet p.21 (illustrated
background), 79; Ben Swift/NB.Illustration Ltd. p.26 (illustrated
background); John Haslam pp.80 & 84 ('the same or different'),
92, 93, 94, 96, 97, 98, 99, 100, 101, 102, 104, 106, 109, 110, 115,
118, 126

Commissioned photography by: Gareth Boden pp.24, 25 (family);
44, 48-49 (Anna and instructor), 68 (people), 72, 73 (having
coffee); MM Studios pp.6, 7, 14 (people), 20 (stallholder),
21 (people), 25 (Jane, Marina and card), 26 (people),
30 (breakfasts for Marta, Paulo and Sakura), 44 (people) 61 (ball
and remote control), 66 (book covers), 81, 86 (breakfast),
119 (Hungarian ID card), 123 (study), 126 (Travelling 1),
126 (Travelling 3); Oxford University Press video stills pp.11,
15, 20 (stall holder), 17 (vox pops), 22 (menu), 23, 27 (Beaulieu),
29 (vox pops), 34 (Rob and Alan), 35 (Jenny and Amy), 39,
41 (vox pops), 47, 51, 53 (vox pops), 58, 59 (meeting a friend),
63 (hotel), 65 (vox pops), 71, 73 (in car, at concert, Royal Albert
Hall), 77 (vox pops)